IN PRAISE OF
WILD
TROUT

BOOKS BY NICK LYONS

The Seasonable Angler
Jones Very: Selected Poems (editor)
Fisherman's Bounty (editor)
The Sony Vision
Locked Jaws
Fishing Widows
Two Fish Tales
Bright Rivers
Confessions of a Fly Fishing Addict
Trout River (text for photographs by Larry Madison)
Spring Creek
A Flyfisher's World
My Secret Fish-Book Life
Sphinx Mountain and Brown Trout
In Praise of Wild Trout (editor)

IN PRAISE OF
WILD
TROUT

Edited and with a Foreword by Nick Lyons

Illustrations by Alan James Robinson

THE LYONS PRESS

Printed in the United States of America

10 9 8 7 6 5 4 3 2 1

Design by John Gray

Library of Congress Cataloging-in-Publication Data
In praise of wild trout / edited and with a foreword by Nick Lyons;
    illustrated by Alan James Robinson.
        p.   cm.
    ISBN 1-55821-671-5
    1. Trout fishing.   I. Lyons, Nick.
SH687.I5   1998
799.1'757'0973—DC21   97-32694
                                                                     CIP

Fifty percent of all royalties from the trade edition of
this book will go to Trout Unlimited and Theodore
Gordon Flyfishers.

CONTENTS

FOREWORD

Nick Lyons

"Stocking fish has been going on so long now in this part of the country," writes Walter Wetherell in "Save the Fountain," of his New England, that "it's become part of the natural order of things, so you have to step back a bit to realize how odd, how truly bizarre the whole business is." He might as well include the rest of the United States. There can be no understanding of wild trout without an understanding of what has been lost, and how, and the difference between a stocked and a wild fish is the touchstone to it all.

With minor exceptions I learned my trout fishing on such fisheries—sluices, really, between one reservoir and another, crammed with the most egalitarian crew of worm-fishers, spin-fishers, and a very few who used flies, harboring mostly trout stocked several weeks earlier, their tails chewed, colors muted, belly and flesh chalky white. Of course we might have had no fishing without those pale shadows of the real thing, the argument might be made, and they would have been the measure of things had we not caught an occasional stream-bred fish, usually undersized and brilliantly colored, or what we called "holdovers," fish of some greater size than the herd and with yellow bellies and bright spots. The holdovers had grown closer to the wildness their birth might have denied, merely by surviving longer in moving water. The closer they came to the real thing the more we loved them. It was not merely that they were larger.

As I grew older and changed my method of fishing from bait and spinner to fly, I wanted more and more to understand the world of the trout stream as well as my quarry, and was less and less satisfied with ugly places and stocked fish; and I understood, more and more, that the quality of the world of the trout and of the trout itself were crucial to my pleasure. In the intervening years, to the poor quality of stocked fish themselves we have added the ills of their cement-trough rearing beds—chief of which, today, is the whirling disease that has already annihilated sections of many of our finest rivers.

Nowhere is the effect of stocking presented with more painful poignancy than in Harry Plunket-Greene's memorable *Where the Bright Waters Meet*. For here we see in the most delightful detail what a river and its bold native trout were—and then the savage decline of the author's beloved chalk-stream, the River Bourne, when thoughtlessly stocked fish, as in Gresham's law, drive out the fine wild natives.

Of course, some of the finest fishing in the world is the result of transplanted or stocked fish (or eyed eggs, which are better)—brown trout throughout the United States, rainbow trout in the East, brook trout in the West, browns in New Zealand and elsewhere throughout the world. Some of the most satisfying, startling fishing I've ever had has been for brown trout in a western spring creek—for fish stocked decades earlier and now acclimated, born to the river for generations, as wild as wild can be. The distinguished Robert Behnke addresses this important issue—and distinction— toward the end of this little book, and it is one that must be made with care and understanding.

What I have gathered here is not a definitive symposium on wild trout but a kind of paean and implied plea—from a quite arbitrary group of fly-fishing writers and poets, with a wildlife-management specialist and a world-class trout biologist thrown in, because poetry and science are handmaidens in this business of wild trout, and the common denominator is that all the contributors love wild trout.

John Engels, our poet, describes such wild trout, brookies in his case, best:

> Little Beaver brookies,
> spotted crimson in pale blue
> halos, spotted lemon
> and white, backs
> moss-mottled-to-black, bellies
> shaded off to a golden ivory,
> fins striped orange and anthracite
> and white—

On such jewel-like fish, often no more than six or seven inches long, "the whole health of our rural culture depends," claims Wetherell, calling the little fish "the quintessential New England creature." That's a lot of weight to put on its moss-mottled back. But beyond theories that such wild fish are the canaries in the coal mine, enough poets and fly fishers live with these trout in their brains that their salvation—and a certain stripe of ours—is worth exploring.

That's what Datus Proper and Chris Camuto do, both writing about Shenandoah Park—and their voices are sufficiently different for me to include two Shenandoah pieces, even in such a small volume; I have not anyway tried to be geologically diverse but to find in these original essays a way to understand the appeal, and the intensity of that appeal, of wild fish. Part of their interest in these fish, and the world of the Park, implies two questions: "What should we leave alone? How best can we protect such trout and their habitat?" The answers to both begin with the affections and end with management and science. They depend upon acute understanding of what such creatures are. "It is tempting to conclude that the real natives are as fragile as the streams they live in," says Proper; but he adds: "They aren't. They are as tough as the oaks, as vigorous as the tulip trees." John Gierach calls the greenback cutthroats of the Rockies "delicate and tough." And he notes: "One of the best things about native fish is that they've often held out in places that are either magnificently wild or at least overlooked."

Such creatures can be protected, as Proper and Camuto indicate when speaking about the management of Shenandoah Park and as Tom Palmer shows in his exploration of how the west-slope cutthroat can be protected and brought back. To do so requires an understanding of what rivers need to sustain such fish—"water quality, sufficient water flows, varying water velocities, cool temperatures, an organic streambed inviting to many forms of aquatic life," cover, the use of contiguous land, sometimes the actual restructuring of a river that man has in some way ruined. In some cases, clearly, it is an uphill climb to restore what has been mutilated—or *is* being mutilated.

But so great is the tug of such wild trout that Camuto can say they taught him "to love wildness," all wildness, and, with his life and his affections, affected his actual choice of a place to live. And Gierach says: "For some of us who live and fish in the Rockies and who appreciate wildness, these are the trout that actually belong here the way we'd like to belong here: comfortably and thoughtlessly." And Proper says: "I have traveled from Montana to fish Shenandoah Park when the trilliums were in bloom." And adds: "Come April there isn't anything I want to do more than watch a green shadow with white edges drifting up under my fly."

I am reminded by such statements of the astonishing ending to Gerard Manley Hopkins's poem "Inversnaid":

> *What would the world be, once bereft*
> *Of wet and of wilderness? Let them be left,*
> *Oh let them be left, wildness and wet; long live the weeds*
> *and the wilderness yet.*

It is such intensity of feeling that animates this little book and that leads me to offer these three practical directives that can help wild trout flourish:

- broad protection of rivers by groups like Trout Unlimited, with national reach and local power;

- better management of land and waters by state fisheries and local conservation groups;

- and what Robert Behnke seeks: "fisheries agencies to shift emphasis from artificial propagation to natural reproduction of wild, especially wild, native fish."

Amen to that.
Let us praise, then, our wild trout—and let us protect them.

SAVE THE FOUNTAIN

W. D. Wetherell

I'm a census taker for our local streams, an unofficial, self-appointed one, someone who likes to keep track of how many wild brook trout still grace our small corner of the planet with their habitation. I go out in all weather, three seasons of the year, armed with the traditional tools of my avocation: an old fiberglass fly rod with three missing guides, a patch of fleece with half a dozen flies embedded in the marl, Polaroid sunglasses scratched and stained from long usage, a scrap of paper, a stub of pencil, and, most important of all, the long and puzzled questionnaire that passes for my brain.

As best as I can determine, there are seven wild brook trout currently residing in our town: three in Slant Brook at the base of a small waterfall where the stocked trout can't bother them; one in Whitcher Stream where it bounces down to the Connecticut; a hundred or so in Trout Pond up on the slope where our mountain begins—trout so tiny, so miniaturized, you could put them all end to end and still only count them as three.

Not many fish, of course, but perhaps the miracle is that there are any left at all. Twenty years ago, when I moved to New Hampshire and began my survey, there were hundreds of brookies in all these locales—enough that the counting of them kept several dedicated census takers working full-time. I'd come upon them in the woods, secretive men apt to shy away at your approach, stubby rods pressed under their arms, their faces greasy with fly dope, favoring dark green work clothes, the only splash of color being the bandannas around their necks. Interesting men to talk to if you found 'em in the right mood; theirs was an intimate association with the landscape and its creatures, and they were less apt to talk about entire rivers or streams than they were individual pockets, boulders, and holes. Most of them valued wild trout greatly, yet possessed one self-destructive habit: they thought of their subjects as food—and not just for thought.

These men are largely gone now. If the trout are down to seven, then the census takers are down to one—me, probably the last one in the neighborhood who realizes wild trout are still among our inhabitants. I've taken to wearing green work clothes myself now, that same red bandanna, honoring by imitation a dying kind of breed. And even I don't go out surveying as much as I used to—I'm tired of walking, knocking, and finding no one is home.

But here I am veering off into bitterness when a census taker should stick to the facts. The trout I know best are the three in Slant Brook. This is as typical a New England trout stream as you're likely to find. Starting high on the side of our town's one steep mountain, it plunges down through the forest in an exuberant rush of brightness, sluicing westward through the uplands, carving a channel for itself through granite bedrock, dropping over two sizable waterfalls and the ruins of old mills, crossing under the highway in a giant culvert, then taking on new life as a meadow stream in the last mile left to it before joining the Connecticut in a marshy bay.

The lower three miles have trout in them, lots of trout, for two weeks a year. These are brook trout that have been raised in cement tanks in another part of the state, transported here by heavy truck, poured into the brook where it meets the road, caught immediately by people who fish no other time of year, the trout that survive being swept downstream by the first heavy rain, to end up as pike and pickerel feed in that marshy bay mentioned above. Stocking fish has been going on so long now in this part of the country it's become part of the natural order of things, so you have to step back a bit to realize how odd, how truly bizarre the whole business is. I mean, phony trout? Cement trout? Trout from the city turned loose to entertain the rubes?

I encounter these trout sometimes in the course of my rounds, and am appalled, not by their meekness, but at their savagery. They strike a fly with desperate fury, turn quickly if they miss and strike it again even harder, as if from an impulse that is homicidal and suicidal at the same time. Catching them, you feel like the butt of a cynical and expensive joke, the kind you see played by art forgers or the worst kind of cosmetic surgeons, those who think beauty is for manufacture and sale. That there is just enough color and energy in these trout to convince the gullible that they *are* real makes the joke more bitter; it's only in comparison to the genuine article that the forgery becomes apparent.

Here's where the miracle comes in. Despite hatchery trout, the nearness of the road, wanton destruction of shade trees, the way the brook's most important tributary is looted for snow-making by our local ski area, the sloppy leach fields of too many houses, the penchant previous census takers had of eating their subjects—despite, that is, every wanton and cruel trick man can play on it, Slant Brook still manages to harbor at least three genuine wild brook trout, huddled together in a thirty-foot stretch of habitat like genuine flowers in the middle of a plastic garden.

How wild trout manage to survive here is partly a matter of luck, partly a testament to what, despite their fragility as a species, is an individual toughness that is as much a part of them as their beauty. A few yards downstream of the looted tributary, replenished by what water trickles in, is a pool no larger than a dining-room table, formed by water falling over a burnished log. A plunge pool you call this—the coolest spot on the brook, thanks to that turbulence, and cooled even more by the shade of a pear-shaped boulder that sits on the bottom a foot or so from the lip of the impromptu weir. Upstream of this there is nothing but shallows for a good hundred yards; downstream are more shallows, so the pool, in brook trout terms, sits like an oasis in the middle of a desert. It's far enough from the road that the stock truck goes elsewhere; it's shady, deep, quiet, forgotten, and in its center live the last wild trout the brook contains.

I've only interviewed these fish, face-to-face interviewed, two or three times. I pride myself on my restraint, claim it's for conservation reasons, but the truth is they're remarkably hard to catch. The stream is hemmed in by brush, making casting difficult. The trout favor the three feet of water between the

4

fallen hemlock and the boulder, so you have a yardstick's worth of drift when they might possibly take your fly. Unlike the stocked fish, they won't rise more than once, and there's much more discrimination in the way they bite—not that greedy boardinghouse grab, but a delicate kind of aristocratic plucking.

They're beautiful, of course, drop-dead beautiful, and already in August have begun to take on that rich purple-red blush that speaks so eloquently of autumn. Only eight inches long, they have the thickness of flank you see in the healthiest wild fish, along with an iridescent luster that makes it seem they are taking the granite sparkle of the brook, the verdure of the forest, the dappled sunlight, mixing it all, internalizing it, then through a magic I never get tired of witnessing, generating these qualities back in their purest eight-inch essence, so holding a trout in your hand, for the seconds it takes to release it, is like grasping nature whole.

The biology of it—how three or four fish manage to survive and reproduce in what is otherwise a desert—mystifies me, and all I can do now is pay tribute to the fact that reproduction, growth, life, does go on here, without any help from man. The Slant Brook trout demonstrate one possibility for the native brookie's future, albeit a tenuous one—living in isolated, forgotten pockets but flourishing there, like cloistered monks working on illuminated manuscripts through the worst of the Dark Ages, their most beautiful, vivid illumination coming from within.

Whitcher Stream, four miles to the south, offers another possibility. Similar in size to Slant Brook, it begins in a chain of beaver ponds in the notch between two steep hills; in time of high water the edges of these ponds lap the rocks of old cellar holes from vanished farms. A meadow stream in its upper reaches, it veers south into our neighboring town, then—as if not liking the neighborhood—immediately swerves back again, finishing its last mile to the Connecticut as a rocky, shady stream with numerous deep pools. Prime trout habitat—and yet to the best of my knowledge, only one trout remains in the entire stream.

It's a native trout; that's the only good news in what is otherwise a depressing enough story. The state stocks only one stream per town, and so any trout in Whitcher Stream is perforce a native. Ten years ago there were hundreds of fish here, two or three in each pool, but each autumn when I went back, there were fewer and fewer, to the point where there's only one left now, in the deepest, most brush-tangled of the pools—a pool that seems, such are the implications, the haunted graveyard where the last of a species goes to die.

I caught it last year and I'm sorry I did. It's an emaciated fish, with the kind of pale, muted coloration you see in creatures who live without hope. This, of course, is anthropomorphism of the worst sort, but there you are—it's impossible to understand what the last trout in a river must feel without taking into consideration what must surely be a cosmic kind of loneliness. For a moment I was tempted to put it out of its misery, break its neck with a little pressure of my hand, but I found I couldn't do this. If the trout in the brook hovered on the point of extinction, I wasn't going to be the one to give them the final shove, or at least pretend I wasn't, me who drives a car, consumes too much energy, accepts too meekly the prevailing order of things.

Nowhere else in town do I feel such a direct connection between the fate of trout and the fate of man. The Whitcher

family after whom the stream is named, among the first set-
tlers here once the French and Indian Wars ended, is down to
one surviving male member—a young man of nineteen who
was just arrested for what in some respects was a meaningless
crime: shooting at a minivan with his deer rifle. He's been sent
off to prison for this; am I the only one in town who senses a
linkage between his fate and that of the Whitcher Stream
trout? Dispossession is dispossession is dispossession, no matter which link on the chain snaps first.

There's lots more here for our local census taker (taking a
break at our village lunch counter, staring down at the one
wretched check mark scribbled down on his pad) to mull over.
Alongside Whitcher Stream, on a grassy level patch above the
ruins of an old box mill, sits an unusual kind of development.
Our local millionaire, as sort of a hobby, bought up decaying
old houses all over New England, had them trucked here, then
reassembled them in a cluster of upscale offices, shops, and an
expensive private school. The backdrop of all this is the
stream—valued for its scenery, its atmosphere, but otherwise
ignored.

The irony of this hardly bears underlining—that so much
effort and money could be poured into rehabilitating a portion of New England's past while the *living* symbol of that
past, the wild brook trout, is left to die out without anyone
noticing or caring. And there are other ironies in this line.
Over on the Connecticut millions have been poured into a
salmon-restoration effort that, sadly, has shown very few signs
of having worked. All this money to bring back something
that's been extinct here for nearly two centuries, and not one
penny spent on preserving the salmonoid that's been here all
along, leaving to future generations the hard task of restoring

it, an effort that will undoubtedly be as futile as trying to call the salmon back with our impotent whistles of regret.

And this, I suppose, is the Whitcher Stream possibility for the brook trout's future: the river as background noise, local color, pretty dead stuff, inhabited only by chub, water spiders, and millionaires.

To write about a third possibility for our local trout I may have to swerve over into magic realism. The eastern part of town is a wild, high province of softwood forest, beaver meadows, and bright open ponds. One of the largest of these is Trout Pond, reached by a half-hour hike along a shaded woods road the years have pressed deep into the earth. Forty years ago the pond was poisoned by the state to "reclaim" it from the trash fish, then stocked by helicopter with brook trout fingerlings. This was a very fifties kind of operation—the helicopter, the faith in technology, the belief in the quick fix. And yet it worked—for a time. When I first moved here and discovered the pond (it's hard to find and the locals kept their mouths shut when it came to directions) the trout had established themselves as a self-sustaining population, and—if you could lug in some sort of boat—you could count on several fat fish over twelve inches, coming up with discrimination to the tiniest of flies.

This was *not* a fly-fishing-only pond; fishermen would dump their bait buckets in the pond when they were done fishing, and a new generation of "trash" fish grew to maturity with those brookies. For a few years both populations maintained a rough sort of balance—and then suddenly, in some ecological battle too obscure to follow, the chub got the upper hand, so they were everywhere, huge ones, attacking a fly the moment it landed so you could hardly keep them off.

As the chub flourished, the brookies declined. I caught fewer each time I went, and found their size was declining, too, so an eight-incher became a real trophy. The good news is that the town obtained control of the pond and saved it from development; the bad news is that no one has the slightest idea how to reestablish the fishery as it once was. Poisoning is out in this day and age, and my own suggestion—backpacking in some chain pickerel to act as hit men on those chub—hasn't won much support either, for the obvious reason: those enforcers are just as likely to eat up the good guys as they are the bad, finish those brookies off once and for all.

What's going on up there is very odd. If you were to have asked me two years ago I would have sworn there were no trout left in the pond at all. I went back anyway last October, lured by the beauty of the pond itself (no mirror reflects foliage better than those three level acres of gray-green glass), and decided, such is the force of habit, to bring along my rod. Someone had dragged in an old aluminum skiff and tipped it against a pine where the inlet comes in. It reminded me of the *Merrimack*—there were bullet holes everywhere, some perilously close to the waterline—but I decided to take a chance. Using some broken hemlock limbs for paddles, I managed to coax it over to the cove on the pond's eastern shore.

I didn't catch fish, not at first, other than those hateful chub. The problem was that my imagination was totally out of sync with the pond's reality; it was still picturing twelve-inch trout, or eight-inch trout, and fishing accordingly. A couple of hours went by . . . I was at the point you can get to too fast in this day and age, when the beauty of the surroundings begins to deflate without some vibrant life at its core . . . when I noticed a vague upswelling in the water by a sunken log—not a rise so much as the ghost of a rise. I searched through my fly box for the smallest pheasant-tail nymph I could find, tied it on with some 6X tippet, then sent it out to see if it could summon that ghost.

It could. Something nudged the wind knot in my leader, then came a tug on the fly itself. I lifted my rod in a reflex gesture—and then ducked as a fish came shooting back toward my face.

This was a lot in the way of gymnastics for a trout that turned out to be two inches long. A brookie, beautifully formed but all in miniature, so for the few seconds he lay in my palm I had the uncanny sensation I was looking down at him through the wrong end of binoculars. Clearly, this wasn't a baby trout but a mature adult—a male, judging by the spawning colors, the vague jut in the underside of its microscopic jaw. I cast the nymph out a little farther and immediately caught another one, a female this time, Mrs. Tom Thumb, just as perfect, just as small. Realizing that two-inch fish were what I was fishing for, I scaled back on my notions, began looking at the pond differently, saw that what I had assumed were the disturbances left by water spiders and caddis were actually bona fide rises—that there were dozens of trout left in the pond after all, at least in this one deep cove.

Good news and bad. Good in that I was pleased for purely linguistic reasons there were still trout residing in a place called Trout Pond; bad in that the race had become miniaturized, so it was hardly correct to speak of them as gamefish at all, but rather as the miniature markers used in a game, toy trout, nostalgic centimeters. And yet I admit I enjoyed catching them, felt these germs of trout create a germ of delight in my eyes, hand, and wrist.

I've been thinking about these trout a lot over the winter. Obviously, the chub are crowding them out, making it impossible for them to find enough food, stunting their growth. But it's hard not to think that the trout are up to a deeper game. It's as if they've deliberately decided, from motives of self-preservation, to become small and smaller, thereby escaping man's attention altogether, to flourish on as a race of midgets no one bothers catching. Trout as leprechauns only the fortunate ever see? Yes, something like this. Philosophers of an earlier age insisted everything evolves toward pure spirit, and this may be the local trout's only salvation, to ruthlessly shut down whatever gene controls growth, evolve into something that is little more than a brightly colored minnow, the bonsai of salmonoids, ignored, unsought for, but at long last *safe*.

Thus my survey, the three possibilities for the familiar neighborhood brook trout of rural New England. Hermitage, extinction, miniaturization—and a fourth possibility I've not explicitly mentioned, but that underlies all my hopes: that mankind (or at least the concerned part of it known as fly fishers) realizes what treasures are on the verge of being lost and spearheads an effort to bring our brookies back, quite literally, into the mainstream of local life.

Census taking, while meant to be a precise science, has built-in limitations, and my methods are not infallible by any means; surveying with a worm, for instance, would undoubtedly result in a more accurate tally, even as it killed my subjects off. Then, too, any census taker, even one who's been at this game many years, has his instinctive biases, and these must be taken into account in digesting his reports. My own bias is this: I believe the native brook trout, the wild brook trout,

Salvelinus fontinalis (which in my pidgin English becomes *save the fountain*) is the quintessential New England creature, the one whose health or lack of health best reflects the health of the natural world here, the being upon whose slender back—not to put too fine a point on it—the whole health of our rural culture depends. Without brook trout, a stream is dead no matter how pretty it looks from the highway; beauty, dead, turns ugly very fast; ugliness, piled high enough, corrodes the soul. There must be a thousand streams in New England capable of supporting wild brookies. Stripped of them, these form a thousand cemeteries, complete with headstones and the keening wail of empty water. Graced with trout, they become springs of delight, reservoirs of solace, fountains of well-being—and not just for trout.

But then census takers aren't supposed to get so involved with their subjects, draw any conclusions from statistics alone. I count, the number is seven, and unless things change dramatically, in a few years the last lonely searcher through these hills will be able to do all his counting on the trembling fingers of one gnarled and arthritic hand.

THE LITTLE BEAVER

John Engels

The turbines at Johnson's Falls
up on the Peshtigo would open,
every morning at seven and the water
would come up three feet in thirty minutes, first
a few twigs and leaves, then a slight
muddying, and then before we knew it
we were having a hard time getting back
to shore, where the rocks and logs

we'd been sitting on an hour before
would be covered, only big V-shaped wrinkles
on the brown surface, and what had been a little riffle
would be a rapids filled with noise
and crazy water. At four

the slots would close, the water fall, and by five

the big river would be a series of clear runs
and riffles between pools. Where one tip of granite
had stuck up, now
a reef of bare rock and sand was drying
in the sun, a few trout would be making
neat swirls near the ledges of the far shore,
and along the banks where we walked
the sweet fern giving off smells
of verbena and sage. So midsummers

what with all the risings
and fallings, I used to give up
on the Peshtigo and seek out
the small rivers, like the Beaver, near Pound,
a little stream, two men fishing it
one man too many, yet
it yielded many a three-pounder,
though to look at it you had to wonder

how such a trout could find the room
to turn around. Try to get to it,
you had to crash brush so thick
you couldn't always get your arms free
to swat mosquitoes and black flies, and once

you came to the water's edge, you like as not
found yourself trapped in some alder hell,
black flies up your nose and in your ears, wood ticks
in your crotch, one foot
on a root above the water, the other
caught in a tangle behind you, or up

to the calf in a mudhole or quicksand, trout
darting away in every direction,
Little Beaver brookies,
spotted crimson in pale blue
halos, spotted lemon
and white, backs
moss-mottled-to-black, bellies
shaded off to a golden ivory,
fins striped orange and anthracite
and white—

Try wading it, you had to bend
double to keep under the arch
of the willows, and there would be
blockades of logs and roots to be stumbled
and scrambled over, and at every step you flushed out trout,

there in the brook like sardines. But finally
I had to give up
on that river, got a cramp

in my back one day, stooping
under the alders, had to crawl out through the swamp
on my hands and knees, was two hours
getting to my car, bad hurting all the way,
out of necessity took to fishing from a boat,
a real comedown I felt it,

going out with Fenske, who
isn't always too certain where he is
or what he's about, one time

when he looked up at the comet
fell over right on his back
in the marsh mud. A man

like Fenske's no good on a river
like the Little Beaver, goddam
pike fisherman, that's what he is,
hardly ever shaves, smells
worse than a skunk in heat,
drunkest man I ever saw,
if you were to give him two dollars
for telling the truth and twenty cents
for lying, he'd take the twenty cents

every time. He used to bring
two tons of gear along in his old GMC
when we went out, his feeling was
it was easier to take it all
than to have to figure out
what he needed. That was Fenske, he had what it took

to make a good pike fisherman—sorry,
Great Northern Pike fisherman. Fish & Game
and the Tourist Bureau people,
what they did was they took our sorry old jack pike
that nobody would carry through the streets
and want to be seen with, and give him
a brand-new name, Great Northern Pike, and made
a million-dollar fish out of him. Wouldn't
of made fifty cents with *snake*, which is what
everybody called him when we was kids. Hell, that's what

I ought to do with carp, Great Copper Bass,
how's that? Make my goddam fortune, which God knows
I could use. One thing I've learned in an otherwise
pretty useless life, the name you give a thing
makes all the difference in the world. Oh, I loved that brook,

the Little Beaver, such beautiful
gliding water. When finally I'd break through to it
at the heart of that awful snarl
of swamp willow, cedar,
alder hell and mud, the world in thickets
between me and the road,
it would be trembling in the sun.

FISHING THE DAWN

Datus Proper

He was hiking down from the Blue Ridge on Sunday morning, trousers still wet from wading and stuck to bony knees, just as sun was burning mist off the mountains. He stood straight. A ghost of red was left in his close-cropped hair, and he talked the way folks in Virginia used to talk before they learned another way from the television set.

He had been born in 1917, he told me, and when he was a boy nobody but him and his brother fished the Run. Shenandoah National Park hadn't been formed yet, so there were no rangers to fuss about whether the trout in a sack were nine inches long. Back then, he said, "a couple of bushels of natives in a pool was nothing." Nowadays, fish were scarce and shy; he'd caught none of keeping size on this early-morning expedition. (A fisherman is entitled to lie about such things if you're brash enough to ask.) He had, however, lost a really big trout that broke him on a snag, up near the waterfall.

He showed me the fly tucked into his keeper: a bee, McGinty-style, with lots of yellow and black chenille and not much hackle. His rod looked about as old as fiberglass gets. His frayed willow creel was a generation older than that. There was no vest, no fly box, no dangling clipper, and no landing net. His whole outfit would have brought maybe six dollars at a Baptist church jumble sale. Still, when he said that he always fished at dawn and cast his wet fly upstream, I would have bet on him to catch more trout than the boys who show up at noon in shiny four-wheel-drive pickups. He made me feel guilty for wasting my time in bed, back in Washington, till 4:30 on Sunday morning.

The other thing I felt bad about was that the dawn fisherman had been wading in a pair of old leather shoes. The rocks were getting pretty slippery, he admitted. He seemed puzzled when I recommended felt soles. He wished me luck, though, and expected I'd need it, considering that the sun would soon touch the water and I was just arriving.

The luck was welcome but the Run saw little sun that day. Shading the pools was a tall young forest of oaks and tulip poplars and hemlocks in early-summer foliage. Those trees had grown big in the years since the National Park Service moved the fisherman's family out of a cove along the headwaters.

His life contained almost all we know of Blue Ridge fishing history. Long before him Indians must have groped for brook trout, but that was prehistory and I've never seen an account of it. The mountains would not have been fertile hunting grounds. They weren't fertile for the immigrants who arrived after 1730, either, and that's why the dawn fisherman's ancestors were poor English, Scots-Irish, Irish, and German. Their life didn't change much over a couple of centuries. They fished without shoes, let alone felt soles, and with a pole and bait—often stick bait (caddis larvae). Hooks were the hardest things to find, but once in a while a fisherman from town would come along and leave a few behind.

Some of the city folks fished with flies. After a summer rain, though, it was hard to beat the mountain boys, who liked to sweep a stream all the way from the Blue Ridge gap down to flatland. The local folks still wait for rains like that and would enjoy them more if it weren't for rangers patrolling the runs.

Of course, in the good old days the fish were all real natives and the streams ran pure. Today, you guess before I say it that the streams are suffering and exotic species have replaced the brook trout.

No. Natives still dominate all of the forty-plus fishable streams in Shenandoah Park, or at least all I've tried. In the lower reaches of some, there are smallmouth bass, which are not native to the area. Brown trout—another exotic—get farther upstream, on occasion, and grow big enough to eat small fish, but I have seen no effect on the population of brook trout, which evolved under pressure from more efficient predators.

Water snakes fatten when the stream shrinks in summer. I started casting, once, to a splash on the surface, then realized that this was no rise-form. A brook trout of about eight inches was half out of the water, held there by a snake four times longer. I thought, briefly, that I should not interfere with nature, then prodded the snake as he crawled out on the bank. He argued but let the trout go, and I flipped it back into the water.

Robert E. Lennon, who studied the fishery in 1961, reported three snakes killing trout simultaneously in one small pool. He

guessed that the trout's large size—relative to other prey—
might have been a factor in attracting the snakes. If the larger
fish are as vulnerable as they seem, it could explain why the
native strain of trout is short-lived (my speculation, not
Lennon's). Few reach lengths greater than nine or ten inches.

High water temperatures were once a serious problem.
Lennon notes a report of trout coping with a temperature
over eighty-three degrees, but that was in 1921, before the
mountain-folks' fields turned back into forest. I haven't had a
reading out of the sixties.

Lennon also reports catastrophic scours in 1954, when a
long drought was followed by torrential rains and flash floods.
Big Run (once the best in the park) was ruined and did not, in
my experience, recover until the 1980s. Other park streams
gave me good fishing when I first visited them in the 1960s.

I have not seen damage on quite the scale witnessed by
Lennon, but in the fall of 1985, a downpour scoured part of
the Rose River, cutting the bed down three feet and destroy-
ing my favorite pools. Upstream and down, boulders and big
trees took the force of the flood. The river in those stretches
was little damaged and trout were abundant (if a little thin) the
next spring.

Floods hit the park again in 1995 and 1996. My first report
on the damage came from Bill Horn, who not long ago was
assistant secretary of the interior in charge of parks and
wildlife. The Rapidan River, he said, was much changed, with
all but house-sized boulders carried far downstream. Despite
the destruction, however, Bill found brook trout of all sizes
abundant.

Park biologist Jim Atkinson was equally encouraging,
reporting some big fish and many young of the year. After

three natural disasters in eleven years, then, the brook trout are doing better than at any time within memory—my memory, at least.

Perhaps the floods should no longer be considered natural disasters. These mountains have, after all, been shaped by the whipsaw of drought and flood. Summers are too hot, rains too erratic, the latitude too low, and the altitude not high enough. Park streams have run low every summer I've fished them, leaving scant refuge for trout in the flats where water flows over sandstone and shale. And then comes the deluge. The mountains are the first west of the coastal plain and must catch the brunt of storms blowing in from the Atlantic.

But the trees have grown back, and their roots combine with hard-rock geology to protect some watersheds. Deep pools are dammed behind hard greenstone ledges. Water cascades over falls and picks up oxygen. Brook trout take refuge, surviving where the contour lines on your topographic map are crowded close together. Geology matters more than hydrology, hard rock more than water.

The trout of the springs, *fontinalis*, evolved here. They are stone green and dawn red, painted by hard rock and nourished by high water. It takes floods to clean the streams, release their nutrients, grow the insects and feed the fish.

Once we almost lost the wild-trout fishery in the Rapidan River, which is the most accessible stream in the park. It has special historic interest, too. Where tributaries join to form the main river, Herbert Hoover built his fishing camp under the hemlocks and spent weekends away from Washington's mosquitoes. If he knew much about fishing, he didn't reveal it in his book, but he got a better trout stream than his successors have in Camp David. His Rapidan camp still stands, well preserved.

In the sixties, Virginia state officials proposed to build holding pools beside the stream, stocking hatchery trout daily to meet demand. People would pay for each tame rainbow. It's hard to believe now, like most old wars. The degradation would have been legally possible, because a loop in the park boundary leaves a good piece of water on state lands—unlike any other major native-trout stream in the area. A road along that stretch would have made it convenient for the hatchery trucks and the sports to get together. Trout Unlimited chapters resisted, and won.

The next threat is coming from the sky. Acid deposition from rain and dry particles has already affected streams running through sandstone, which has a low buffering capacity. Most of it is in the southwestern corner of the park, below Highway 33.

Granite has an intermediate buffering capacity and has, so far, protected streams in the east-central section of the park, including the Rapidan. Basalt buffers best, protecting Jeremy's Run, Piney River, parts of Big Run, and several others.

The dawn fisherman's big trout was right where he said. I sneaked up on a wide, flat pool, but before I could get in casting range, a brown of about sixteen inches spotted me and cruised into the cleft of a boulder the size of my car. I rose from my knees and a second brown, bigger than the first, followed it into shelter. Those two were the only uninvited guests all day, and I didn't want to spend time entertaining them anyhow. They would have been approachable only in dim light—as I'd been warned—but the brook trout in the smaller pools and pockets were just getting active now.

The first fish of the day came from the run at the head of the big pool. From my knees I cast the leader over a green-stone ledge and watched the V-shaped calf-tail wings on my little Coachman. They drifted slowly, with no drag, and winked out in the cautious *plip* that sizable brook trout make. This one was in peak condition, and no eight-inch trout could pull harder. There was more suspense than you might expect: if I had let the fresh fish change its angle of pull abruptly, the fly might have come loose.

This trout came lively to the net, deep sides glistening with red spots and blue aureoles. In the air, he was almost gaudy. Underwater, nothing had showed but the white edges of his fins.

Many of the fish in these streams are yearlings, which must be returned. Two-year-olds are also common, and under good conditions a number of those will be over eight inches in length. (They have already spawned once.) A few exceed nine inches. A very few are three-year-olds, not much longer but big-headed and showing their age. This is, in short, a population that renews itself quickly. Growth rates are good by comparison to those in other brook-trout streams of the mid-Atlantic area. Shocking surveys (and my own experience) show that spring populations are almost identical in the Rapidan River—which has no-kill regulations—and in comparable streams where trout over nine inches may be taken. The Rapidan's fish are neither more abundant nor larger in size. This suggests that the nine-inch limit is giving the trout all the protection they need.

It is tempting to conclude that the real natives are as fragile as the streams they live in. They aren't. They are as tough as the oaks, as vigorous as the tulip trees, and as fruitful as the hemlocks. Despite the dawn fisherman's complaint, these waters often have about as many fish as they can hold without stunting. I love them. I love these little trout more than two-pounders in Argentina, where good fishing isn't a surprise. I have traveled from Montana to fish Shenandoah Park when the trilliums were in bloom.

It is not customary to credit humans for good work in nature, but let's do it this time. Those rangers wouldn't have to spend rainy dawns on Big Run, guarding against illegal fishing. And the hills could have been left to developers fifty years ago. It's easy to guess what might have been, because today most of the trout streams become sucker streams within yards of the point where they flow out of the park. The difference between good fishing and none is the National Park.

It is possible to be overprotective, too. There are people in the National Park Service who would like to put an end to fishing: perhaps not all at once—the protests would be hard to handle—but by looking for ways to squeeze the regulations tighter and tighter.

There are two levels of fishing in the park. Not many anglers realize how difficult it is to catch the good two-year-olds consistently. Most drive up, fish for a couple of hours, hook a few yearlings, and reckon they've done what is to be done. That leaves the real fishing for you and me. We have two choices.

The easy choice is the Rapidan—the only stream with good access by road. This is the best bet for beginners, families, groups, those who would rather drive than hike, and those who just get lonesome. That's the disingenuous way to put it. Here's the other way. I feel about a busy stream as the villagers felt about the czar: Lord bless him and keep him—far from me. Maybe you don't share this aversion to crowds. Be aware, in any case, that the trout learn, and you won't catch the big ones many times in a season.

The other choice is to walk. You'll catch more fish, perhaps even more good fish, and find privacy. But—especially after the first part of the season—you may have to put a couple of miles behind you. The easy way is to leave your car at the lower park boundary and hike upstream. The prettiest and steepest way is to hike down from Skyline Drive, which gets you into a few streams inaccessible from the bottom.

Next you find that you can't fool those big eight- to ten-inch fish. They drift up under your fly, give it a professional critique, and drift back down. Or maybe they don't even give you a rise. They fail to appreciate that you got up early, drove for two hours, hiked for one, and would now like some coop-eration from innocent wilderness brook trout.

Well, maybe *you* can do it, and sometimes I can, but there have been humility lessons. The big trout today come from ancestors that learned to reject suspicious flies. By taking slow learners out of the gene pool, anglers are creating a race of brookies as suspicious as the browns, who got a long head start. I have had to fish longer and harder for nine-inch Shenandoah fish than for the big Letort browns (and big in the Letort means about fourteen inches). It's not the stereotype of the brook trout.

The fishing can be easier from mid-April through May—sometimes. On April 13, 1985, a mile from the nearest road, the water was perfect but even the yearlings were tough to catch. The eight-inchers would not show. I slowed, changed tactics, exhausted each bit of holding water, abraded my knees on the rocks, skipped my lunch. The sun rose overhead and dropped behind the hemlocks. At the end, I had landed four colossi—meaning trout over nine inches—but only one in the eight- to nine-inch range. What had afflicted his peers? A February flood two years earlier at hatching time? Drought? Snakes?

Bill Horn. I called him at his office in the Department of the Interior to complain about the trout under his supervision. He should, I said, reduce their pay and demote them to dace. Instead, he told me of a coincidence. He had fished the same stream the day before me. He had covered it faster than I did but had included most of the same stretch. He had caught eight trout between eight and nine inches long, releasing most. They learned fast, and I learned why those puzzling bad days occur.

Early in the season, while the water is high and clear, the small streams are at their peak. I haven't fished them all, but so far each I've tried has been good on its day—except for those in the sandstone area. Lists with rough directions are available from the rangers at the entrance stations, and the concessions on Skyline Drive have the maps you need. The trout won't be in peak condition yet, but they'll take either nymphs or dry flies well. At the beginning of April their stomachs will have big stonefly nymphs, crayfish, salamanders, the occasional small fish, miscellaneous floating insects, and maybe the odd Quill Gordon nymph or dun. But don't stand around waiting for a real hatch. You could wait for a couple of years.

When the water levels start to drop, usually in late April, you may do better on one of the bigger streams, though all see a lot of fishermen—especially near the access points at the boundary. At this time, beetles and black flies are important food.

Sometime between late May and July the water is likely to get so low that even the steepest parts of the big streams become difficult. You can still catch fish, but they separate the men from the boys, and most of us boys move to the Pennsylvania limestoners, or to Montana. Appalachian fishing improves with the cooler weather of fall, but you still need a rain to raise the water. When the leaves change color and redds appear in the streams, I don't disturb the trout. (It's an agreement we have. They don't bother my marriage; I don't bother theirs.)

In Shenandoah Park streams, then, a fisherman's first concern is with water levels. It's hard for a western angler to learn that fishing is best during the runoff. It's hard for an angler from limestone streams to grasp that he must understand water, not hatches. As the levels drop, though, the fish change their lies, and the main problem in each weekend's fishing can be finding the new places.

I can sometimes catch more Shenandoah fish on deep-sinking nymphs than anything else, but I get more of the sizable brookies on dry flies. The difference is that I can cast a floating fly over a rock and let it wander around on a loose tippet. The boulder has been there since the last flood and will wait till the trout makes his mind up. The rise, when it comes, is visible and I have a good chance of hooking the trout. With nymphs, I can't hook fish unless I keep the leader reasonably straight, and that moves the fly along faster than the big eight-inchers like to make decisions—let alone the trophy ten-inchers.

Then again, maybe I'm inventing reasons for doing what I want to do. Come April there isn't anything I want to do more than watch a green shadow with white edges drifting up under my fly.

GREEN BAY FLIES

John Engels

Two deep rivers ran
    through the heart of town to the Bay,
and in March I watched the ice break up
and the big floes go tumbling, splintering
the piers, debarking the oaks and pines
along the banks four feet up their trunks.
In April, the first thunder
in six months, proclaiming
spring, and in July
up from the Bay, from beyond
Peet's Slough and Long Tail Point
and the marsh meadows blue
with sweet flag the hatch came,
a fly or two fluttering

to the street lights, then a few more, then
before you knew it
the mayflies of Green Bay would be swarming up
the Fox in huge rustling clouds half as wide
as the river, so many they darkened the arc lights
on the Blue Jays' field, covered
every window pane, clustered the screens, clogged
car radiators, covered your hat, your sleeves,
sometimes even brought traffic

to a halt. You could feel their wings
brushing your face with little breezes
that I swear were enough
to cool you down on a hot night, the air
adazzle with wings, and high
in the evening sky swallows
by the hundreds, cedar waxwings
darting out from the trees to meet a fly
just perfectly in midflight, one second
this little fluttery dab of golden light,
then the flash and hover
of the bird, then

nothing,
like a flicked switch, the evening gone
minutely the darker for it.
If it had been raining
the streets and sidewalks in the morning
would be slippery with a green slime
of eggs, the flies having mistaken
the wet concrete for a surface
of live water. But nothing

like it anymore, the hatch
is over, probably
forever, the Bay a soup
of silt and sewage and sulfides
from the mills, not even clean
enough to swim in anymore. But back then,
those summer evenings—I can still
hear it, the sound
like a long train
way off in the distance,
a sort of humming rumble
wrought up by those millions,
billions, of delicate wings

that caught up every last scrap of light
left to the day in that last
half hour as night came down
and the street lamps
came on. I've never forgotten
how it was those years in July
the night stepping in, slow

and deliberate as a heron, the sky
softly darkening like it does
even now, evenings
in late summer, a smell
of lawns and dust and the steely
scent of the Bay drifting in, the air

still hot, but a growing softness
to everything—at such a time

you could surprise
yourself, catch sight of yourself
in a shop window, if the time
was right, and the mayflies
hadn't yet swarmed the glass, and depending
on how you wanted to look to yourself,
in such a light you'd look it.

CUTTHROATS

John Gierach

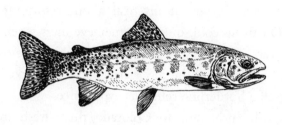

Among the half dozen or so standard questions fly fishers eventually get around to asking each other is, What's your favorite fish? Some say your answer to that will be deeply revealing—exposing you as a covert aristocrat if it's Atlantic salmon, a closet bubba if it's largemouth bass, or whatever— while others just think it might be interesting, but sooner or later, in one way or another, the question comes up.

For the longest time I thought I was fickle because I hardly ever gave the same answer twice in a row; it was brook trout one time, browns the next, and maybe bluegills the time after that—whatever I'd caught most recently. But then I realized I was giving the right answer to the wrong question. The fact is, it's fishing with a fly rod I'm stuck on, but I'll pretty much go after anything that doesn't have legs, and my favorite fish could be a carp if that's what's taking line off my reel at the moment.

Still, like a lot of fly fishers in the Rocky Mountain West, I have a real soft spot for cutthroats because they're our only native trout. When I first started fishing for them, some people around here still called them just that, natives, and knowing only that, it was possible for me to hike miles into some pretty little alpine lake in the wilderness area, catch a few ten-inch cutts, and get downright mystical about returning to the source. On those cool, quiet summer evenings when no jets passed over on their way to the old Stapleton Airport in Denver, I could drink the few warm beers I'd packed in and have myself a borderline religious experience.

I was still fairly new to Colorado then: fresh from the Midwest, young, innocent if not plain dumb, and prone to fits of romanticism, so naturally I was disappointed when I learned that the cutthroats in those mountain lakes weren't native in the finest sense of being the direct descendants of the ancestral fish.

But then the best guess from most of the experts was that there were no ancestral fish up there. Most of the high-altitude lakes along that stretch of the East Slope, they said, were separated from the lower waters by natural barriers and were fishless when the West was settled. The trout in them now are the results of early, haphazard stocking—official and otherwise.

A fisheries biologist once told me that in the old days anyone with a bucket or a milk can could get a load of fingerling trout and put them wherever he wanted to, and that the first plantings done by the Division of Wildlife itself weren't much more scientific than that. The result on the one hand was that a lot of already depleted native cutthroat fisheries were destroyed altogether by the introduction of brown, rainbow, and brook trout. On the other hand, some thriving fisheries were established where before there had been no fish at all.

You can apply revisionist criticism to all that if you want to—asking, Why didn't those dumb schmucks a hundred years ago know what we know now?—but the fact is, it was mostly done with a good heart and, in some cases, the kind of monumental effort you only see from people convinced they're doing the Good Work.

For instance, many of the trout in my neighborhood wilderness area were planted by an old private club that packed fingerlings in on horseback and, now and then, on the strong backs of volunteers, for no other reason than that it pained them to see pretty mountain lakes with no fish in them. They even went to the trouble of stocking cutthroats. They were Yellowstone cutts—native to the region, though not to the state—but, given the information and the hatchery stock available at the time, that's a pretty fine point.

If there had been cutts in those lakes a century ago, they'd have probably been greenbacks. Greenback cutthroats were thought to be extinct by the late 1930s, but then the legendary Dr. Behnke at Colorado State University located a small, pure-strain population in a little creek near here, in the high headwaters of what was once their native range, and now they've been introduced into a dozen or so lakes, streams, and beaver ponds in and around Rocky Mountain National Park. You can fish for them on a strict catch-and-release basis (presumably, few people now living know what a greenback tastes like) and, although they may not have existed naturally in those particular waters, they would once have been found only a few miles downslope, and that's probably close enough for government work.

I think the first pure-strain cutthroats I knowingly caught were greenbacks, and that's only because some people who really knew told me that's what they were. The same fisheries guys say some of the cutts my friends and I catch in the more remote streams in the area are wild greenback-Yellowstone hybrids (the old fish crossed with the more recently introduced ones) and that in some cases they may even be "virtually pure" or "grade B" greenbacks.

To be honest, I can't always tell the difference between a pure greenback and a closely related pure Colorado River cutthroat, or either of those from the hybrids, and, when it comes right down to it, neither can most of the fishermen I know. The different races of cutthroat do have their distinctive markings—the spots on a greenback are bigger than those on a Colorado River cutt—but the kind of ironclad identification you'd be willing to swear to is just beyond most of us.

Still, greenbacks are highly regarded around here. After all, they're a once-thought-to-be-extinct fish that you can now go and catch, which amounts to a rare environmental miracle. Another miracle is that they were brought back by a recovery team made up of several state and federal agencies that cooperated for a long time and in the end actually accomplished something worthwhile.

And they're just a delightfully wild fish: surprisingly delicate in some ways and just as surprisingly tough in others. For instance, they're so unused to competition that they'll be crowded out by almost any other species of fish, which is what happened to many populations of them in the first place. But then when you look at that tiny little creek where they held out until they were rediscovered, it's hard to imagine trout making it through a single winter there, let alone countless winters.

It's just a little trickle flowing through an aspen and willow bog, and if it weren't for the Division of Wildlife NO FISHING

signs you wouldn't even know it was there. But if you find a
tiny pool and crawl to the lip of it on your belly, there they are:
miniature, jewel-like trout with impeccable pedigrees.

And they say the recovery team had a lot of trouble raising
them in a hatchery because, among other things, the greenbacks refused to eat commercial trout food. You've got to
admire that.

So anyway, I had a little crisis of faith when I found out the
first cutthroats I went to so much trouble to catch weren't quite
what I thought they were, but I got over it. I mean, it wasn't the
worst case of lost innocence I ever had, and I did come out of
it with the regulation western affection for cutthroats in general, not to mention respect for the tough old birds who humped
those particular fish in on their backs in the first place.

Since then I've caught real Yellowstone cutts in the Yellowstone River a few times. (By "real" I mean pure-strain, native
fish living in their historic home water.) I've usually ended up
doing that around Buffalo Ford in a god-awful crowd of other
fishermen, but the trout were big and lovely and they had
flawless bloodlines, so it was still a rush.

Once some friends and I hiked a long way into a high
mountain valley on Colorado's West Slope—on a tip from a
biologist—and caught what we were told were pure-strain
Colorado River cutthroats. None of the fish were very big, but
they were living in the stair-step beaver ponds and connecting
channels that meandered down one of the prettiest little high-
mountain meadows I've ever seen. There were wildflowers,
snow-capped crags, and a stand of ancient, hundred-foot-tall
Engelmann spruce trees that had either been missed by the old
logging crews or, more likely, left because they'd have been
too hard to get out.

I remember there was a black trout in one of the pools. Not just dark, but black as a burnt stump. None of us could catch it.

I have two snapshots from that trip. One is of my old friend A.K. holding a fat, foot-long cutthroat and grinning like it was a hundred-pound tarpon. The other is of Ed, casting to a perfect little beaver pond while standing in a field of wildflowers. I guess it was classic. One of the best things about native fish is that they've often held out in places that are either magnificently wild or at least overlooked.

A few seasons ago I caught some pure Snake River cutthroats from a big reservoir in southern Colorado. That was also a beautiful spot, though in a different way. It was flat, brown, treeless, windblown, and, on that particular trip, cold as hell and downright lonely: the kind of place where one good, drunken country-western tune on the car radio could permanently break your heart.

Once again, I know they were pure-strain fish because a fisheries expert with whom I would never argue told me they were. What struck me was that they were damned big trout, and I noticed that on a real pig of, say, five or six pounds, the normally fine, tightly packed pepper spots sort of spread out, as if they'd been painted on a balloon that had then been blown up.

Just in the last couple of years I've gone several times to a drainage in British Columbia that holds native westslope cutthroats. One of the rivers we fished last summer is glacial in origin, with glass-clear, bluish-green-tinted water and a clean, light gray, bare rock bottom. The cutts there weren't pale exactly, but they were subtly colored, muted, well camouflaged.

But then one of the little tributaries to that river apparently had a completely different kind of water chemistry. The water was still clear, but the bottom was thick with dark aquatic vegetation and so slippery you could lose your footing in an ankle-deep riffle. The fish—still pure westslope cutts from the same drainage—were deep green on the back with greenish pewter sides, jet-black spots and brilliant orange gill covers and cutthroat slashes on their chins. The three of us had split up for a few hours to try out the little creek—even our guide had never fished it—and when we met back at the truck we all said in unison, "God! Did you see those fish?"

I don't think this gut affection for cutthroats is any great mystery. It's just that for some of us who live and fish in the Rockies and who appreciate wildness, these are the trout that actually belong here the way we'd like to belong here: comfortably and thoughtlessly. The same can be said of brook trout in parts of Labrador, Guadalupe bass in parts of Texas, and so on. Native fish look, smell, and taste of a place just as, to a fisherman, that place looks, smells, and tastes of the fish.

Okay, fine, but if the trout at the end of a long uphill hike turn out to be a grade B strain or the wrong race for the drainage, well, I'm a mutt from somewhere else, too, so maybe I shouldn't be too critical. I mean, my hometown hybrid cutts have a kind of romance all their own. Maybe less than a tepee ring, but every bit as much as an old abandoned trapper's cabin. After all, things are seldom perfect and perfection itself may be overrated, but life can still be good.

Cutthroats are just a kick to catch, especially when they turn up unexpectedly, as they still do now and then. Even a cutbow—the cutthroat-rainbow hybrid—can give you hope that there's still a little wild juice left in the old river system. And if the cross happened in a hatchery before the fish were stocked, okay, but I don't want to hear about it. We're talking about symbolism now.

Just about everyone I fish with gets inordinately excited about catching cutthroats, and they'll mention a surprise cutt in detail in the first few sentences of the report on a new stream: "We caught browns and rainbows to about fourteen inches, and one cutthroat. He was eleven inches and had that red belly stripe like a greenback. Took a size sixteen Elk Hair Caddis."

Sometimes news like that will make you want to go back to the same stream and go higher yet, looking for that secluded meadow stretch or headwater lake past the place where the rainbows or the brookies give out and it's either all cutthroats or no trout at all.

I still do things like that—though not quite as often as I used to—and, although I admire almost any fish that will eat a fly and I have a new favorite after every trip, catching a cutthroat still gives me that mindless don't-confuse-me-with-facts buzz I got as a kid.

It's not a matter of symptomatic relief. Some of my favorite writers who have talked about trout fishing sometimes imply that it saves them from the big-time, high-pressure craziness of their lives—like a good, strong sedative. I sort of know what they mean and, although this ain't exactly the big time, I do know what craziness is. But I have to take one more step back from that. I'd say fishing saves me from needing to be saved—sometimes just barely.

And it's not that I'm out to recapture my past, either. In fact, there are some episodes from those days I wouldn't mind forgetting altogether. And anyway, what was it Tom McGuane said? Something about how it's bad enough for a writer to "visit" something in the first place, let alone to "revisit."

I think the same goes for recapturing. Over the years I've held on to that old simpleminded enthusiasm, knowing that once it's gone, it's a waste of time trying to get it back. I don't know how I know that, I just do.

THE NORTH BRANCH

John Engels

We took the train in Lakewood.
There'd been fires in the old days, swept
the North Branch country,
but over the years we fished there
most of the land recovered itself
in second-growth popple and wild
cherry, scrub maple
and birch. Blackberry
and raspberry bushes got thicker every year
in the clearings, and in the shadow
of this shrub, here and there, you saw

seedlings of hemlock from the few
remaining stands, even a few
white pine that came

from god knows where. And fern, may apple, winter-
green, coral mushrooms, *russula,*

and everywhere you looked
stood the charred stumps of the old pines,
some of them too big for the two of us
to join hands around. Made you wonder
what it must have been like

before the fires and lumbermen. It was
hard country
around that river,
killing frosts

by the middle of September, in October
snow began, lasted
six months, by the third week
of April you might see
a little grass again. When my brother
and I fished those rivers

we found a farmer let us sleep
in his hay barn, we'd pull together
a four-foot mound of hay
and sink into it, and get waked up
by the mice stirring in the hay,
and know by that it was daylight
and time to get up. No rats, thank god,
big pine snakes underneath the barn,
saw them lots of times
sunning themselves on stumps. Used to be

that river was something, read once
in the files of the old *Green Bay Advocate*
of a party took seven hundred
and eleven trout in three days
of fishing. This was

at the end of August, 1871. Another time
some years later four hundred
and sixteen fish that ran
a quarter pound to two and a half. Nothing
like that anymore, of course, and of course
that's why. But I tell you

it was still a beautiful stream,
the North Branch, in the upper reaches
wild, but lower down
a river for swans, maybe
forty feet wide, in places, and running deep
between the banks, and a powerful

current, so that even in the glides
it was punishing to wade
upstream, and then below the highway
it spread out in
a still water, but still

with lines of drift that went
past us quicker than we could wade
or walk the banks. We'd come
to the stream with the wet brush
in our faces, and sometimes we'd stand

on the meadow bank below
the oxbow and see
little grayish blobs of insect shapes
bobbing to the surface and fumbling

themselves airborne, and twenty feet out
the neb of a trout showing and gathering
one in, and then a hatch or spinner flight
filling the air, swallows by the dozen
hawking among them, cedar waxwings
coming out of the trees to take
one fly, and every square yard
of the stream with a feeding
trout. Black flies
could be bad, especially around

the pilings of the cattle bridges,
crawled down your collar, into
your ears, up your nose, your cuffs, bit
like a sunuvabitch, I used to think we'd maybe lose

a pound of meat apiece to them
some days. But we'd stay at it
no matter what, until almost sunset,
when the chill at last got to us,
and we'd come off the stream
shivering, bleeding, exultant.
In those days that was a river
where unless hot prairie winds were blowing in

from Kansas, or the Fox
had opened the reservation dam
and sent down a head of muddy water,
we felt we could take fish

somewhere along it—even
on the worst days we used to take
a lot of brookies in the riffles, small,
but by god they'd brighten the day!

CAUGHT BY THE WAY

Christopher Camuto

*From ancient times wise people and sages have
often lived near water. When they live near water
they catch fish, catch human beings, and catch
the way. . . . Furthermore there is catching the self,
catching catching, being caught by catching, and
being caught by the way.*

—*Eihei Dōgen, "Mountains and Waters Sūtra" (1240* A.D.*)*

I think of trout as an affair of landscape—not something *in* it,
but something *of* it. In Chinese, the term for landscape, *shan
shui*, means literally "mountains and water." Roughly speaking,
if you rub a mountain with cold, flowing water, you get a trout.
This is to take a compressed view of geology and evolution,
but mythic and scientific ways of thinking about things converge
in extraordinary expressions of being, like trout. Of course, I

51

refer to wild, native trout in free-flowing mountain streams, not manufactured fish or trout spawned in the artificial rivers that leak apologetically from the base of dams. Wild trout in their native landscape are part of a strong, distinctive expression of the spirit of a place, whether we are talking about Apache trout in the White Mountains of Arizona, goldens in the high Sierras, or *Salvelinus fontinalis* here in the Blue Ridge. If you don't find native trout where mountains and water clash, then the surrounding landscape falls apart downstream of its empty headwater in the same way that the idea of the Great Plains fell apart without the buffalo and eastern North American skies once paled in the absence of peregrine falcons.

When I moved a few years ago from the eastern side of Virginia's Blue Ridge mountains to take up residence in a hand-hewn log cabin on the western slopes, the first thing I did was explore the rivers near my new home to see which held populations of wild brook trout. "In a strange place," writes the poet John Engels, "the first thing / is to look for running water." The next is to head upstream past the bream and bass, then past the tepid stretch of river where hatchery trout mill about, continue into second-growth woods and good water and miles of wild rainbows—handsome but not native—until the first enraged brook trout grabs a cocky Adams Quill under the closed canopy of a true forest and does its Celtic war dance at the end of your line, tying you to the water and to the mountains in a way nothing else could, catching you. This warrior is likely to be five or six inches long, but it's a perfect expression of the singular form of life that tells you that this little headwater stream is still *alive*.

I hadn't moved very far—I was perhaps a hundred miles southwest along the Blue Ridge from the rivers I had fished hard and well for ten years. But the bedrock cradling west-slope streams are, in most places, not the acid-buffering, bug-producing granite and basalt over which I had happily learned to fish for wild, native trout before I knew how rare they were. And I had been spoiled by the fact that my favorite trout streams were protected by the sheltering confines of Shenandoah National Park rather than exposed to the "multiply-used" realm of the George Washington and Jefferson National Forests, where my fishing had to compete with bulldozers, logging trucks, ATVs, and other Forest Service denials of what a forest is. (It's the trees, stupid.) But I knew that in the mountains it's best to suspend judgment and poke around, and as I worked my way from stream to stream, there were as many pleasant surprises as disappointments.

I found what I most wanted, and needed, a forty-minute drive away—an intact watershed with mountains and water and wild trout and just about everything else that implies: gray squirrels, fox squirrels, grouse and turkey, deer and black bear, and if not "painters" then at least memories of panthers in stories I got from the human natives of the place, who gathered ramps and morels and ginseng with the same quiet passion with which I fished and hunted. At first the locals looked on my fly fishing with frank, if friendly, pity. But the frequent appearance of my battered F150 with a tag from a neighboring county earned me some credibility. Eventually several backcountry walkers with whom I crossed paths suggested that if I was fishing for natives, I should lash a "lizard" to my hook. I didn't doubt that a wriggling salamander would do the trick, especially in the plunge pools that might harbor a fourteen-inch square-tail, but I was the one trying to get caught, and the flies I tied in winter and cast in spring were part of the offering.

These mountain acquaintances—wise people and sages following a way of the life in the mountains—came to understand
that I was practicing some magic of my own and eventually
accepted the unnecessary complications of my fly fishing as
part of some necessary ritual, my chosen way of being there. Of
course, a fourteen-inch brook trout was exactly what I wanted,
and in my dreams I fished with lizards.

This mountain stream became my new home water and its
watershed my prime hunting grounds. I also sketched there
and sometimes just watched the life of the place. I fished and
hunted according to rules of engagement I had invented for
myself—a wisp of a fly rod for trout, a slender flintlock long
rifle for squirrel, a well-balanced twenty-gauge muzzleloader
for grouse, and an 1858 Enfield for backcountry deer. This last
choice may well be the most poignant firearm in American
history. I imagine that more than a few Civil War veterans,
Confederate and Union, brought one home, carried it into the
woods, and tried to collect themselves around the old idea of
their hunting. Possibly too much had changed for such men,
within and without, and maybe gunfire was not what they
wanted, nor killing, and they spent a lot of time just watching
the life of the place.

I didn't take up hunting until I was in my thirties, as a way
of getting further into the woods I had grown to love as a fisherman. My hunting derived from my fishing, and to pay one
practice back with the fruits of the other I filled my mountain
fly box with the fur and feathers of fall. Grouse lived on in soft
hackles, deer in caddis and humpies, squirrels in buggy
nymphs whose wing cases were fashioned with bits of turkey
feather. Continuity mattered more than sophistication. But it
all came back to the trout, which centered my backward-

seeming ambition, tugging my heart and mind into the heart and mind of the mountains. Without wild trout, I would have moved on elsewhere, not just for the fishing but for the hunting as well.

Like the strange rivers that drop from the mountains in Northern Sung paintings, my mountain stream comes in and out of view, and this quality winnows out interest in it among most fishermen. It is not unusual for Appalachian streams to secret themselves underground for stretches, testing the loyalty and persistence of the curious. A mile upstream of the last dirt turnaround where you can park, the river forks deceptively. What looks like the weaker, less productive branch at the confluence—a shallow dribble of water over broken slabs of bone-dry shelf rock—was, a mile farther up the mountain, a far better brook-trout stream than the main flow, where rainbows outnumbered the brookies until that branch was too small to fish with pleasure. My first fall there an otherwise unproductive day of grouse hunting revealed a prime mile of spring-fed brook-trout water tucked up on the mountain above a steep cascade that apparently fended the rainbows off. The only bird I flushed that day broke cover as I leaned over the tail of a leaf-strewn pool of umber autumn water with my twenty-gauge at port arms. Six hours out, I was footsore and tired and for a split second thought, in fatigued surprise, that I had flushed a trout into the woods. I marked the spot in my mind and followed up the grouse, which I never saw again. On the way back down the mountain, my empty game bag felt like an empty creel.

This spot where my hunting and fishing selves crossed paths became a center, and eventually I took both trout and grouse, once on the same day, within a hundred yards of where, shotgun in hand, I first saw good-sized spawning brook trout finning over a clean gravel tail-out. Now every autumn I cruise the nearby hardwoods for small game, keeping an eye out for a fox squirrel with the tawny shades I prefer for my dark streamer flies. I chase grouse in the hemlocks along the stream and, up on the ridges, through recovering clear-cuts. I make backcountry deer camps along that upper reach during the early and late muzzleloading seasons, pursuing a fine eight-point buck I saw ghosting through bare timber one foggy morning the first December I hunted there. I've never seen the ghost buck again, but that whitetail is as useful to me as the fourteen-inch brook trout I've not yet caught.

Bracing the long barrel of the flintlock against a tree, raising the straight stock of the grouse gun to my shoulder, or waiting silently in ambush with the Enfield, I'm still tethered to the wild trout that drew me into the mountains in the first place. That trout stream remains the wandering baseline of the time I spend in its watershed, the feature in the landscape from which I take my bearings. As a practical matter, its branching tribs, most dry half of the year, lead me to the squirrel haunts and grouse cover, and I can follow them safely in the predawn dark to a backcountry deer stand. The stream keeps me from getting lost, and anytime I feel like being a fisherman again, the trout are there, sages themselves, the wise *roshi* that caught me by the way and taught me to love wildness.

Against the background of the shifting seasons, the stream tumbles through the year. By the end of grouse season in early February, it may well be encased in ice and the surrounding woods knee-deep in snow. The deer, grouse, and squirrels are so skittish by then, they are as remote as the invisible trout, and for a few weeks the stream and its surroundings are a perfectly empty stage. At home I disassemble my old-fashioned guns, cleaning them well—lock, stock, and barrel—and tie flies tainted with bore butter with fingers stained brown with stock finish. I fashion dry flies in the sparsely hackled but buoyant Catskill style, making my own slight revisions to fit the sizes and shades of our southern mountain hatches.

Hiking along the stream in midwinter, I absorb the fact that the topography of its watershed is as clear as it will be all year. Rather than fish the river before its time, as I used to do, I have taught myself to draw the stark forms of bare trees and bedrock in winter, to sketch shed antlers and rifled caches of walnuts and, of course, the river itself. I've learned to relish that cold, hard hiatus between the hunting and fishing which seems to invite the practice of other arts. Walking in winter, you see the underlying idea of the place—mountains and water.

The world around the trout stream is born again in March as rotted snow melts and the battered woods slowly come to life. Bloodroot push up through the leaf litter and open on sunny days like flags of truce; maples and alder, serviceberry and sweet birch flower and leaf in. The oaks and other hardwoods wait overhead with open crowns. Migrant passerines feast on the run, torn between hunger and their wild, inspiring desire to travel. The hard-changing river of early spring is often unfishable, but the water clashing off the rocks revives the idea of trout that will soon take just as hard. That vision keeps me at the tying desk for hours on rainy days, attending to details I know wait in the coming season. From my front porch I can nurse a cup of coffee and watch the rain in the mountains. My work at the vise gets finer each day as my fingers get nimble with practice. In the evenings I root around in old fly-tying books for new ideas. By the time snow peas have sprouted in the muddy garden, that mountain fly box is full, from Quill Gordons to sulfurs, nymphs to spinners, and the river has settled down enough to expose windows of fishable cover along the lower, broader reaches.

This early-season fishing is more like hunting, a fish or two enough to confirm that the universe is intact and that its more important laws are still in force—for example, that wild trout take dark soft hackles in slow water in early spring. If the delicate emergers don't work, I grease the tip of the fly line and the butt section of the leader and short-line heavy nymphs through the hearts of pools, dislodging trout from bedrock one by one. Near midday, bathed in sunlight, I lighten and lengthen the tippet and cast dark Quills upstream of rising fish, striking quickly at the rumple where the fly disappears. For a few weeks, I feed last season's birds and squirrels to the trout, fly by fly, and feel the seasons, and the years, pulled taut.

In April the still-boisterous water seems to encourage hurry, but it's best to wade like a bear and fish slowly, moving a bit behind the day, doing justice to the winter deliberation you practiced at the fly-tying vise when you wound the stiffest hackle you could afford on the delicate dry flies you now need to float like corks. As the sun warms the water and stirs the early-season stoneflies and mayflies that stir the trout, you can give yourself over both to intuition and to the physical pleasure of fishing. In the end, it's stealth that catches trout. And stealth, when fishing or hunting, is style—your way of being in the river or the woods. For being in the river, Charles Cotton's advice remains the best: "Fish like an Artist and peradventure a good Fish may fall to your share."

The good fish are where they should be—rainbows in the white water, brook trout in dark, syrupy seams of current. You can tell what you've hooked by feel. Even in a small stream, rainbows fight like western fish, making runs to the heads and tails of pools, as if they remembered longer rivers. The brook trout thrash stubbornly in place, as if this were their turf. Mountain trout are hungry, not gullible, and each spring gives the lie to the myth that these trout are not selective. Still, they don't pick and choose with the serene patience of spring creek browns. My mountain fly box mimics things well enough, and each year I'm pleased to see how well I've matched the life of this rocky, free-spirited water.

The rest of spring is easy, and the fishing effortless in a way hunting never is. Once regular, if sporadic, hatches begin— sunlit bursts of duns here and there—I work my way upriver as the rushing water settles down, reacquainting myself with each stretch of woods, spending whole days leaning into the stream lost not in thought, but in the repetition of my craft. Wade, wait, watch, cast, retrieve. Puzzle out the current and the lies. Mend line to keep the fly alive. Stop before you fish each pool or riffle, breathing deep to fill your lungs with mountain air. Feel the woods off either shoulder. Observe any- thing that moves as a sign of the year revealing itself to you but turn back quickly to the fishing. Study the undersides of rocks like a raccoon to see which pale, watery green nymphs have matured. Watch the surface of the water, and the air, for winged insects. As the day emerges, tie on longer, finer tip- pets—enjoying the minor discipline of tying a proper blood knot—and then reach out to the river, bowing to it as you strip line in quick retrieve. Rustle a fly box out of a vest pocket; choose a fly that fits the moment from a trout's point of view.

Watch the pool you've just rested during these chores. Cast and retrieve, bowing. Then wade on, leaning into the river, working your way up the mountain with the strange, stately progress of a wading fisherman.

By mid-May the brook trout have grown fat and strong again. The cold mountain water preserves traces of their spawning colors, autumn passion paled but not obliterated by a winter. The rose of the rainbow darkens. The seasons are lap-jointed in these two species of trout, as well as in the frost-cracked boulders beginning to simmer, in the way the forest canopy flowers like the forest floor. The river tunes itself to its rocky bed, rising and falling with the immediate weather, practicing a more subtle art as time wears on. The trout, wild at heart, shift around between the water and the rock shadowed by a heronlike fisherman—the tiny figure in the Sung landscape—who casts and, retrieving, bows, casts and bows.

Sometime in June, when the flowing water slows and warms, the trout begin to mill around what pools remain in the river's summer self. The inviting riffles are gone. The woods have closed. Before the weather turns stifling, I'll walk the watershed, bottom to top to bottom again, a twelve- or fifteen-mile loop, depending on the way I choose. Most watersheds in the Blue Ridge are man- or woman-sized affairs. One long day's traverse will give you a good view of the whole, of which a day's fishing or hunting is only a part. It's five miles to the modest crest of the Blue Ridge the way I like to walk. I follow the familiar river for three miles, through its hemlock-cooled hollow. Then I break faith with the river's way, jagging off across a ridge of chestnut oak and chinquapin as if I were after grouse. That ridge takes me to a saddle from which I hunt deer in winter. There is no view in summer, but a boggy spring, around which club mosses thrive, that vents a barely audible trickle into the woods which I could follow, as the deer do, to the river and the trout.

A short steep pull will bring me to the Appalachian Trail, a welcome presence that gives me solidarity with many another walker who loves the thin country of eastern wildness. A few miles southwest, I cross a series of toe-deep, spring-fed flows that are the very headwaters of my river. A detour takes me to an outcrop of lichen-encrusted granite, picketed by mountain ash and Catawba rhododendron. From this raven's view of rock I can survey the entire watershed, study the shape of its wildness—a long green dent of valley and ridge—admire how finely formed and note how finite it is.

The lay of the land—from that, everything else springs. Wildness from wild places. Mountains and water.

In autumn, when I have a rifle or shotgun tilted over my shoulder, I'm shunned by hikers and backpackers. I get hard looks or muttered rebukes flung at my back, insults I've never drawn while leaning over the meat case at the supermarket. But for some reason fishermen are figures of innocence, even though they too may intend to kill their prey. Along the lower stretch where a maintained trail converges with the stream, hikers will stop, spook the fish in the pool I am working, and happily ask about the *fishing*. I tell them pointedly I am *trout* fishing. To a man, and woman, they seem to like that—*trout fishing*—and I can see myself rise a notch in their estimation from the fool they thought I was. If they linger, I try to work in, proud as a father, that the stream is full of wild, native trout—my way of saying that the world is in good shape here, that they have picked a fine place to hike even if they aren't fishing—but most sense a specialist's jag coming on and shuffle off along the trail before a full-blown lecture or, worse, a sermon starts up. They have their own passions—black-burnian warblers, lady slippers, mountain laurel, or just love of the woods and the day itself, time spent in a wild landscape between mountains and water pursuing in their own way the path of wise people and sages.

Innocent as I may seem with a fly rod in hand, twice a year I allow myself a meal of wild trout, a brace of brook trout in the spring, two rainbows in the fall. I do this to remind myself that this is not a game. Catch-and-release fishing is an ecological necessity, not my preference. The practice smacks of bad faith, an inauthentic act. In hunting, of course, you cannot call the bullet back, and that may well be why the wildness of trout led me to the wildness of the hunt. In any event, the bounty in this watershed is real and you need to take it, and taste it, now and then, like a profane sacrament—the world's body. Fly fishing among the well-heeled sportsmen on famous, crowded rivers has become both too expensive and too cheap. Too much a sport.

Perhaps these dark mountains make those of us who love them a bit too somber, but it's good to remind yourself that you cannot really undo what you've done in life, let the consequences of your actions simply swim away, as if nothing had happened. Slipping a trout back into a river may be a wise gesture, but it is not necessarily a virtuous one. Here in the Blue Ridge, life is small-timey but *dear*. Slitting the silken belly of a trout, for an important meal of wild food, is as strange and serious an act as rolling the heavy viscera of a whitetail deer onto the ground or pulling the delicate entrails from the body cavity of a still-warm grouse. With the blood of fish and game on one's hands, a very clear idea of the cost of living forms in the back of the mind—and stays there.

Still it feels good to let most trout go, just as it feels right at times to let a grouse hang in the air until it's too late to pull a trigger. The release cuts both ways. Perhaps it's not bad faith. And there's something to be said for showing wild trout to people who have never seen one, as well as for watching the splash of surprise on someone's face when you open your hand and let the incomparable fish disappear in the green water.

I once crossed paths with a student of mine when I was knee-deep in the river. I was teaching that fall, as I sometimes did, at a nearby university. She had been walking the trail that followed the lower stretch of the river which was popular with weekend hikers. Cigarette in hand, she could hardly be called a hiker. She was casually well dressed as she always was at school, not in the preppy garb of her peers but like a woman who was already making her own way in the world and had no need of a uniform. A very promising painter, she had talent, she knew it, and she hid her fear of the strange fire in her art behind a pleasant haze of ironic detachment. Tall and slender and elegant, she made her most drab peasant dress urbane. She reminded me of someone I once knew.

Beautiful young women in peasant dresses don't stop to converse with middle-aged fishermen, even though that may be every middle-aged fisherman's dream. When I hailed her, she laughed to recognize the rube in the river and graciously sat down on a streamside boulder as if it had been put there for her use. She offered me a cigarette, a standing joke between us.

Unhappy with small-town college life, she was transferring in the middle of her sophomore year to a school in New York City, where *she* was a native. She missed the sights and sounds of urban life, the kaleidoscoping impressions that fed her art. She said she wanted to *go* to college, not live *inside* of one. As bright verbally as visually, she had written a brilliant essay for me on the Puritan poet Anne Bradstreet, writing full of graceful insights that would have snapped heads back in graduate school. I was sorry to lose such a student, but I wrote a strong letter of recommendation for her and was glad she was trusting her instincts and following the demands of her art.

She seemed unimpressed with the river and the woods, but since I had taught her American literature with wit and passion, she granted me the benefit of the doubt and looked at the water flowing around me as if there might be something in it.

"So this is *trout* fishing." She knew my prejudices.

With her sitting there coolly hugging her dress around her knees, native skepticism gathered, trout fishing suddenly didn't seem like much.

"And where are the trout?"

Trying to match her aplomb, I casually flicked a tiny Adams to the head of the pool and, pagan though I am, earnestly prayed to God—any God—for a trout, a gorgeous wild brook trout.

I played the fish enough to calm it down and, cradling it with my hand in the water, brought it to her.

"*Salvelinus fontinalis,*" I announced.

The brookie was broad enough in the flanks to bring out its full design. Add to that its flagrant autumn colors and even this young sophisticate—as they say in novels—fairly caught her breath. She was surprised, as everyone is, first at the primary colors that came out of the drab river—that odd galaxy of red and blue aureoles—as well as with the shocking orange, then with the forest-green tracery of vermiculation on the fish's back, and finally with the incredibly high-contrast black and white of the finely wrought fins. I held the brilliant fish just in and out of the water, keeping it wet and bright. She didn't poke at it the way people do. She studied it.

"You see the highlight in its eye?"

I hadn't, though I'd seen a thousand trout.

She nodded and smiled when I let it go.

"*Salvelinus fontinalis*," she intoned.

There was a highlight in her eye, too, where I hoped I had put a painting. Perhaps someday I'd see it hanging in a gallery or, better, a museum. Not some diligent rendition of a brook trout, or some smarmy sporting scene, but a strangely natural abstract image—some telling metamorphosis of the color and form of a wild trout the artist had once fixed her brilliant, dark-eyed gaze on.

I've been nearly ten years in this new place. Now it's dead midsummer again, too hot for fishing, too hot for anything but night walks and stargazing. The dog sniffs out traces of quail in blackberry thickets while the Perseids spark overhead. Later, after invisible clouds obscure the sky, I sip green tea and admire the ancient floodplains of Ares Vallis on the computer screen in my study, pleased to have an austere new world to contemplate. Mountains without water: variations on a theme in the solar system.

Near midnight, watching the arid Martian landscape assemble itself on the monitor, I can hear thunder in the nearby mountains making trout.

TROUT HABITAT IN THE BLACKFOOT COUNTRY

Tom Palmer

Ten years ago, Don Peters, a fisheries biologist for the state of Montana, grabbed his coffee cup and began to trek up and down the Blackfoot country's 1.5-million-acre watershed in search of a landowner who'd offer him a refill. "I didn't know it at the time, but what we're doing here is ecosystem restoration," Peters told me. "That's what this is. We're doing ecosystem restoration and we're doing it across the coffee table with the people who own the land."

The Blackfoot River drainage in west-central Montana, an area that would cover nearly all of Delaware, is the site of an immense river-basin restoration effort that began in 1988. It had an odd start. Blackfoot River fishermen were not catching the fish they once were. When they convinced officials they knew what they were talking about, Montana Fish, Wildlife & Parks agreed to try to determine why wild trout were getting harder and harder to find. By 1990, Peters's ensuing study had found dwindling numbers of wild trout over the entire length of the Blackfoot River. Toxic mining wastes and tributary streams degraded by timber harvests and livestock use had profoundly affected the Blackfoot's ability to produce even reasonable wild trout populations. Especially hard hit were the Montana natives, westslope cutthroat trout and bull trout. Both wild fish are today a fin flutter away from a federal listing as threatened or endangered species.

Since then, a lot of coffee beans were ground to restore more than two hundred stream miles in twenty-three tributaries, reestablish fifteen hundred acres of wetlands, patch up fifteen thousand acres of upland prairie, and acquire conservation easements on more than forty-five thousand acres of private agricultural land. All to restore trout habitat and reestablish watershed wetlands. "We're still learning how bad it was," Peters said.

With this project, Peters and others have managed to bring under the tent a slew of state and federal agencies, land and water conservation groups, a timber company, a power utility, wild trout activists, duck hunters, and local ranching families. "The problems are still there," he told me early one summer morning outside Trixi's Saloon, a Highway 200 roadhouse that sits atop a hump of glacial till between the North Fork of the Blackfoot River and the Scapegoat Wilderness. Peters came out of the barn-red saloon a bit sullen. The barkeep had turned down his request for a cup of coffee. "She's not open yet," he moaned. He peered across the highway to the watershed's Scottish kettle and kame landscape whose lush green hues shone in the morning sun. "It's not all fixed," Peters said, managing an almost cartoonish gap-toothed grin. "We're not done. We may never be done, and we're still ten years away from seeing any results. It's a hell of a thing, neglect is."

It is true from sea to shining sea. We have been told with numbing regularity that America's rivers and the elaborate support system of soils and plants that make our watersheds have been gut-shot. And a gut-shot landscape is no place for wild trout.

Wild trout need plants to grow along the stream. It's a basic fact of salmonid life. Depending on where they live, they need little willows, big cottonwoods, and old-growth timber. This woody vegetation amounts to a pantry that contains a wild trout's whole grains and chokecherry juice. High flows and swollen waters spilling across the floodplain create the growing conditions for willows and cottonwoods. Trees and shrubs sprout from the newly deposited silt and sandbars that emerge once the floodwaters recede. These flood-dependent streamside plants help create a subterranean macramé of roots and knurled knuckles of roots and wicker baskets of roots that embrace the good soil and fortify the stream bank. A riverine system that isn't faithfully cloaked in trees and shrubs is one not bound to support wild trout. Trout need those plants, shrubs, and especially trees to die and decay and fall into the water. Fallen trees mark the points in time where simple flowing water begins to muster the health and energy to become a wild trout stream.

"The Blackfoot system was sick," Peters told me. "Logging screwed it up. Mining screwed it up. Ranching screwed it up, and it died because there wasn't any wood in it. If you go to a forested stream and there's no wood in it, there's something wrong."

In fact, there is a direct relationship between wild trout populations and the abundance of aquatic insects, branches, decaying leaves, logs, tumbleweed-sized root wads, and snags in the stream. But with anywhere from 70 percent to 90 percent of this nation's natural riparian vegetation lost or sadly degraded, it's becoming a real stretch to consider wild trout at all.

But consider them we do, even in ragged, weary, and simplified ecosystems. We have simplified our riverine systems by changing the water quality, diminishing flows by irrigating our crops, damming, draining, dredging, and straightening our rivers, filling our wetlands, and feeding our streams a steady diet of an eroding landscape brought on by a hunger for burgers, timber, and urban development.

Our simplified ecosystems have been hit with planetary strength Liquid-Plumr. From Oregon to New York the quick drain-away results have turned the natural complexity of a wild trout's place within a biological system into outdoor aquariums, and the conceptual ideal of the well-stocked stream have made us all rubes in the swindle.

For wild trout these are basic: water quality, sufficient water flows, varying water velocities, cool temperatures, an organic streambed inviting to many forms of aquatic life, and the shape of the stream itself. Together with gravity these basic attributes create places cut by flowing water that provide habitat for trout at different stages in their rather brief lives. If you cut off the tributaries from the river, straighten stream meanders, chop down the trees, allow cattle to pound the banks, and build a suburb on the floodplain, you've made a mess of wild trout habitat.

On the ground wild trout habitat looks like trees, and shrubs, and lots of branches hanging over the stream, shading the water. The stream banks are stable and the water might generally be about five times wider than it is deep. The streambed is relatively, or at least regularly, clean of muck that embed gravels and cobbles. Pools and riffles recur in section after section, and subaqueous weeds and plants and bugs waft and drift with the currents.

Good trout habitat ought not to be too much for any cold-water stream to hope for. Within the Blackfoot watershed the hope hinges on fixing the riparian areas along tributaries to the river's middle reaches. And the work is being done with an understanding that trout spawn in a particular type of habitat, grow in another kind, live as adults in still another, and spend the winter in yet another kind of habitat. Once upon a time it was a simple complexity, and it can become so again. But to piece the story back together one must think about several narrative layers.

Trout-spawning habitat consists of clean gravels where steady, moderate flows of cold water continually supply oxygen to the eggs and wash away any potentially smothering debris. Spawning habitat can be limited in steep streams, as in the Blackfoot drainage, where the gravels are carried from the hills and only boulders and cobbles are left behind. In the valley, spawning can be similarly limited due to silt and sand deposits moved from the hills. Most redds—trout-spawning nests—are found just above a riffle or just below a pool, where the female trout begins the herculean task of building the redd by clearing the gravels, depositing her eggs, and then covering the eggs with gravels after they are fertilized by the male. In *Better Trout Habitat*, Christopher J. Hunter shows that spawning needs vary by species. Rainbow trout and cutthroat trout mirror the spawning scenario offered here, but brown trout build redds in cover-protected habitats and in places where upwelling springs bring more oxygen to the eggs. And, once they've built it, brown trout will come back to the same redd year after year. Brook trout spawners seek colder waters than either brown, rainbow, or cutthroat trout and are more critically sensitive to the early environmental stress of pollution than are brown trout and rainbow trout.

Once hatched, all trout need what has come to be called nursery or rearing habitat, a misnomer because trout are neither nursed nor reared by other fish. They are, however, nursed and reared by the habitat itself, which must provide protective cover and slack flows or glides in the side channels and along the margins. Trout fry will struggle to survive in a hard-charging mountain stream that has few pools and eddies, and they will struggle to survive in a stream that offers ideal flows but no streamside cover for protection from predators or shade to cool the shallow, slow-flowing water.

Within a year of egg fertilization, nature can take a serious toll on wild trout populations. While yearling survival rates can vary tremendously, some studies have shown that only 5 percent of the wild trout spawned even in superb habitat survive their first year. In *Native Trout of Western North America*, Dr. Robert J. Behnke reports that a female trout can produce up to two thousand eggs per kilogram of body weight, but a stable trout population can be maintained if only two progeny from a pair of spawning fish survive to reproduce themselves. These second-year trout are those fit enough to hone their long-term survival skills, skills that are defined and shaped by their habitat. They'll migrate from the nursery to the kitchen—the insect-carrying riffles—then immediately seek out territories in deeper pools created by fallen trees locked in the channel, or beneath a suitable shady bank, or behind a boulder.

Adult trout finally establish themselves in territories that are a mix of slow, deep waters near fast-moving currents that shuttle food to them, and where nearby cover is provided by logs, boulders, root clumps, overhanging grasses and branches and undercut banks. These habitats serve two needs: protection and something fish ecologists call "visual isolation." Visual isolation is created by breaks in the topography of the streambed. The breaks are supplied by instream plants, the turbulence of riffles, logs, boulders—any number of things that hinder one fish from seeing another in the stream. It is important because trout are fiercely territorial. If one wild trout spots another in its feeding station, it will mount an immediate offensive to oust the interloper. Size and aggression naturally determine the victor, but if trout are not visually isolated within a stream's segmented territories, too much energy will be expended on territorial defense and too little on the simple pleasure of instream life. Stress develops, and the defeated trout drifts downstream to places that probably offer an even more stressful existence.

This is essentially the problem that occurs when domestic hatchery-reared trout are dumped on top of wild trout. It's not that hatchery trout are piscatorial hoodlums; they just do not share the wild trout's penchant for visual isolation. An essential aspect of wildness is missing. Territory is an issue for hatchery trout, but it seems they really don't know why. It's as if hatchery trout have acquired an attention deficit disorder. Some studies have shown that hatchery trout stocked in wild trout waters blunder into established wild trout territories and then blunder back out, suggesting that hatchery trout make no connection between the shape of their new environment and the manner in which they live their lives.

Layered on these narratives is the major conflict that is now building to a resolution in the Blackfoot watershed: wild trout survival is affected by the health and condition of the watery realm, which is dependent on the health, condition, and use of the terrestrial landscape. Or, as Peters observed once he began to install fish screens on irrigation ditches within the Blackfoot drainage, "We fixed one and then we found we had to go down to the next ranch and fix that one, and then down to the next one. Pretty soon we figured we had to fix them all."

I wanted to get a closer look at the work so, near the end of the summer, and after an unusually wet season marked by floodwaters that threatened to blow out expensive and labor-intensive stream-rehab work, Peters invited me up to visit Rock Creek.

Rock Creek, the main tributary to the lower North Fork of the Blackfoot River, cuts a channel historically formed by a braided glacial outwash. In 1991, Rock Creek was a wide, shallow stream. It lacked wood, pools, and instream cover. Several stretches ran bone-dry, and sutured channels blocked free-ranging fish passage. Irrigation diversion structures, culvert crossings, livestock grazing, bald stream banks, and riparian timber harvests had sucked the life from Rock Creek.

Peters nonetheless believed Rock Creek could be brought back to health, that it could again serve as a spawning and rearing stream for westslope cutthroat trout and bull trout. He coffeed with landowners up and down the creek's eight-mile meander and convinced several ranchers to allow him to remove six barriers to fish passage. In turn he replaced two ancient water diversions with headgates of a more efficient design and found the funding to convert wasteful flood-irrigation systems to conservation-minded sprinklers. The rehab package effectively increased stream flows for wild trout in Rock Creek. That done, trout habitat was further enhanced by narrowing the channel, adding woody debris—trees, root clumps, and such—and planting riparian shrubs and conifers over the entire length of the project.

That summer day, the rehab section looked like a beat, narrow snake of a stream with banks of mud. A sod of native grasses was just again beginning to green up after an entire growing season spent under floodwaters.

Peters walked carefully along the soft banks, examining the sawed-off cottonwood stubs. "Hey, look there. A toad!" The delicate mud-colored amphibian was about the size of a quarter. It hopped idly across the mud bank and plopped into the creek. "There's another one," Peters cheered. "This is good. This is good."

The sawed-off cottonwood stubs looked like proper firewood logs sticking straight out of the mud. Many had green shoots sprouting from the white bark. "Hey, look at this," Peters shouted. "These cottonwoods are growing. Oh, my. Will you look at that!"

Western historian Dan Flores has suggested that our national conservation themes over the past five or six generations fall into two classifications. The theme of the late nineteenth century upheld the idea of public retention and management of natural resources. The twentieth-century theme has revolved around preserving select pieces of the natural world. The theme of the twenty-first century, Flores believes, may well be that of restoration.

While it is important to preserve and maintain the best of what's left of our diminished natural landscapes, a restoration theme for the third millennium is one wild trout activists ought to embrace. We need a Marshall Plan for restoration that seeks to restore not what we think once existed in a natural state, but what could be called the possibility of ecosystem health based on the condition of our watersheds, beginning with the health of our rivers and streams.

Some years ago I heard environmental historian Arthur F. McEvoy say that human culture changes as people accumulate experiences through working in nature, but as people use that learning to get the things they want from nature, they really begin to make nature over in their own image.

That's exactly what Peters is doing, climbing about the Blackfoot watershed in his search for landowners with coffee on the brew. "For too long people like me have been problem describers," he told me. "We'd see a problem and we'd chart it and we'd go back out there year after year with a fish shocker in our hands, when we should have been walking up to the porch with a cup of coffee, trying to get to know the rancher who owns the land." By inviting landowners to take another look at their lands, Peters is luring them away from their own cultural version of visual isolation and asking them to make the connection between the shape of their new environment and the manner in which they live their lives. The people involved in the Blackfoot restoration have begun to recognize the natural limits, and they are working with nature in a new way, learning that they can get what they want, to hold to the land. In the Blackfoot country, trout-habitat restoration is caught in the root wad of what is essentially a lifestyle issue. Ranchers want to stay on their land and anglers want to catch wild fish. By imagining a better way to live in the world—tomorrow's world, and not the world of the late nineteenth century or the twentieth century—they are piecing back together an entire watershed with a wild-trout-habitat template.

"The success of individual projects is important," Peters's team wrote in the Blackfoot River Restoration Progress Report. "But even more important is our willingness to work with landowners who will try to incorporate land-management practices more sensitive to ecosystem health."

Since the work on the Blackfoot watershed began, bald eagles are expanding their territories, and numbers of nesting pairs are up. Black terns are in the drainage, and no one recalls ever seeing them before. Today, there are twenty-eight nesting pairs of curlews in the uplands, a brand-new development of the most welcome kind. And now ten years into a still evolving project, westslope cutthroat trout and bull trout numbers are increasing in some of the restored streams.

After my tour of Rock Creek, I made my way upcountry to fish the North Fork of the Blackfoot River. I wanted to fish just below the Jacobsen Ranch, where Peters worked to establish an elaborate system for keeping native trout in the river and out of the irrigation-canal abyss. I walked a half mile downriver before crossing. I marveled at the clarity of the water and how well I could distinguish the size, shape, and speckles on the multicolored river stones. I threw a Joe's Hopper to the shadowed seams that ran below the undercut banks, but with no takers.

At the first river bend, I climbed up on the trunk of a fallen tree to cross the river again and entered a shady and serene stretch of water. Cottonwoods lined both banks. Through the trees I could see honey-colored bales in the hayfield sun, and at the tail of a diamond-blue pool I saw a fish rise. I don't rightly know why, but when I saw the rise I recalled what my twelve-year-old son, Ryan, asked me only days earlier. "Dad, you love rivers, don't you?" What a wonderful thing for a son to think of his father. He loves rivers. I'm not at all an accomplished fly fisher. Not even close. I don't have the intensity for it that I see in my friends who are exceptional anglers. After several unsuccessful casts with several different dry flies, I tied on a small, pale white Irresistible. I cast upstream to the head of the pool and watched the fly drift under rust-red skeleton branches reaching up from the water. The tiny fly crossed the pool and was taken lightly by the trout. I set the hook and immediately felt the heft of something powerful and real. After several minutes I had the fish within reach. I removed the hook without lifting the fish from the water, then watched a bright blur of a vigorous westslope cutthroat trout return to the pool. I do love fishing for these wild creatures because it puts me in the water; it takes me to the river where trees have fallen soundlessly, reverberating the eternal return of wild trout for longer than anyone can remember.

WILD TROUT AND NATIVE TROUT: IS THERE A DIFFERENCE?

Robert J. Behnke

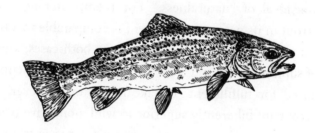

For conservation purposes it is important to fine-tune the definitions for wild trout and native trout. The term "native" or "native born" for humans commonly means that a person was born in a certain country, state, or some geographically designated area. For all other species of animals and plants, however, "native" means that the occurrence of a species in a particular geographical area is the result of an ancestor coming there naturally (not transplanted by humans). Once transplanted outside their native range by humans, (for example, rainbow trout in the East and brook trout in the West) the species will always be a nonnative species.

The term "exotic" means introduced from a foreign country. The brown trout is an exotic, nonnative species in North America, where it has been highly successful in establishing wild populations. No trout, nor any species of the family Salmonidae, is native to the Southern Hemisphere; thus, all wild brown and rainbow trout in New Zealand and South America are exotic, nonnative species.

For most anglers who make a quality distinction between wild trout and hatchery trout and have no concerns whether wild trout are native or not, the matter of precision of definition might seem irrelevant. There are a few anglers with a romantic ideal of "naturalness." For them, catching a rare native trout in its native environment is comparable to a book collector obtaining a rare first edition. In both cases, knowledge of subject matter and a deep appreciation of authenticity is required for fulfillment. I make no claim, however, that native trout are inherently superior to wild, nonnative trout.

A more pragmatic reason for concern for native trout and salmon relates to the preservation of the diversity of adaptations. This mainly pertains to diversity among races and populations within a species (intraspecific diversity). Much of this diversity has already been lost. The American Fisheries Society has determined that 107 distinct races of Pacific salmon, steelhead, and coastal cutthroat trout are extinct and more than 200 other races are in serious decline. Adaptive life-history differences among populations or among groups of similar populations, called a race, can be quite great. Steelhead and rainbow trout are two different life-history forms of the same species, *Oncorhynchus mykiss*. Both forms may occur in the same river, where young steelhead smolt and go to the ocean and undertake a journey of thousands of miles, returning as large adults, whereas members of the resident rainbow trout population live out their lives in a small stream at a small size. In the same river, steelhead and rainbow trout are so closely related that even the most refined genetic analysis cannot positively separate them. Yet, somewhere in the largely unknown portion of their hereditary material, different codes initiate strikingly different life histories. The September 1997 listing of certain steelhead populations to be protected under the Endangered Species Act is an example of the current awareness of the importance of preserving what's left of the range of diversity in the species *O. mykiss*.

This awareness of the importance of preserving all of the parts of a species, or at least the remaining parts, is a relatively recent phenomenon. How people perceive nature and how this perception is translated into public policy by government agencies has an interesting history that explains much of the loss in diversity of our native trout and salmon.

In the nineteenth century the prevailing concept in relation to nature and natural resources was of humans dominating, subjugating, and controlling nature. In agriculture, nonnative and, especially, exotic species were regarded as good, valuable species to be spread around the country. Also in agriculture, there was a belief that species could be "improved" under domestication and cultivation. When brook trout were first artificially propagated in 1853, the hatchery craze began and rapidly expanded to initiate a naive faith in the technological fix to right all wrongs and solve all problems.

The U.S. Fish Commission was established in 1871. Its mission was to restore and increase the abundance of food fishes. This was to be accomplished through hatcheries and by transporting "valuable" species to all parts of the country, to waters where they did not occur naturally. One of the commission's first large enterprises was the outfitting of a railroad car as an aquarium car in 1873 to transport hundreds of thousands of freshwater and marine fishes, shellfish, and lobster from the East Coast to the West Coast. This first attempt at a transcontinental shipment of such magnitude came to an inglorious conclusion when a flood weakened a trestle over the Elkhorn River in Nebraska, plunging the whole train into the river. Nevertheless, within weeks, a shipment of fewer fishes arrived safely on the West Coast to promote the introduction of nonnative species.

In 1877 the U.S. Fish Commission began rearing carp shipped from Europe (an exotic species), and soon began shipping this "valuable" fish all over the country. The carp is now the most abundant freshwater fish species, in terms of biomass, in the United States, but perception of its value has changed. In 1875 and again in 1884, the official policy of the U.S. Fish Commission was stated in its annual report. The tragedy of the commons was becoming apparent in commercial fisheries, especially the salmon fishery of the Columbia River. Unregulated fishing was leading to overexploitation, and pleas were made for regulation so that the salmon fishery could be sustained into the future. The stated policy of the U.S. Fish Commission was to make "valuable species" so abundant that there would be no need for regulation of catch (the carp could be cited as a successful example of this policy). This was to be accomplished through hatchery propagation. Thus began the massive hatchery propagation of salmon and steelhead that continues to this day.

Unfortunately, large-scale artificial propagation was based on an erroneous concept of a species. It was generally assumed that all members of a species are essentially the same, like so many standardized interchangeable parts. In reality, the abundance of anadromous salmon and steelhead depends on maintaining a great diversity of races and populations. This hereditary diversity is maintained by spawning fish homing to the streams where they were born. This prevents the mixing of populations and allows for site-specific adaptations to evolve. For example, chinook salmon or steelhead that migrated seven hundred to a thousand miles for spawning and whose offspring migrated to the ocean over the same route would have distinctly different life histories than populations of the same species spawning ten to twenty miles from the ocean. How many distinct groupings of chinook and steelhead originally occurred in the Columbia River basin is a matter of speculation. Three distinct populations of chinook salmon with different life histories occur in the Nanaimo River on Vancouver Island. The Nanaimo River is only thirty miles long; its watershed would have to be multiplied several hundred times to equal the original salmon spawning area of the Columbia basin. The nineteenth-century large-scale propagation of chinook salmon established a central hatchery. Each year, many millions of eggs were taken from many spawning populations in the Columbia basin and from populations outside the basin. All were mixed together, and the newly hatched fry were stocked out into many waters. This forced mixing of locally adapted populations to produce a homogenized, generic stock of a species is now known as outbreeding depression—the loss or dilution of locally adapted populations by hybridization.

Coho salmon and steelhead were also subjected to forced mixing and outbreeding depression by the methods of artificial propagation. Even into the 1950s, when dam construction was widely under way on the Columbia River, the technological fix was again invoked, with the building of new hatcheries to give the illusion that "we can have fish and electricity too." We now have a better understanding of how a species can be made up of many different parts that are not interchangeable, and that abundance of a species depends on maintaining its intraspecific adaptive diversity. For many of the parts of our native species of trout and salmon, it's too late: they are gone.

From the above, it should be clear why there is an important distinction between the terms "native" and "nonnative" and that "nonnative" also applies to the mixing of populations of the same species in hatcheries, leading to the loss or dilution of locally adapted populations.

Besides lower abundance due to poorer survival of "homogenized" hatchery trout and salmon, other hereditary factors, such as maximum age and size and resistance to disease, can be altered by stocking nonnative hatchery fish into waters with native populations.

For about twenty years a research project has been going on in the Kalama River, a tributary to the Columbia River in Washington. This long-term study was designed to answer the question, What impact does the stocking of hatchery steelhead have on native steelhead? The Kalama River has both native winter and summer runs of steelhead and has long been stocked with both winter- and summer-run hatchery steelhead. Genetic markers allow for estimating the survival rates of both hatchery and wild fish. Survival differences vary from year to year, but a long-term average is that when hatchery steelhead survive to spawn, their survival from egg to returning adult is only about 10 percent that of the wild, native steelhead. Obviously, if much interbreeding occurred between the native and the hatchery fish, outbreeding depression and reduced survival would result. Fortunately, the hatchery fish spawn at different times and somewhat different places, so that inter- mixing is minimized.

The Metolius River in Oregon, a tributary to the Deschutes River of the Columbia basin, had been heavily stocked with hatchery rainbow trout for more than seventy years. The native rainbow trout of this region coevolved with a micro- scopic parasite, *Ceratomyxa shasta* (a parasite related to the one that causes whirling disease), and hence have a natural resistance to the infection, which is lethal to trout lacking resistance. When compared with native rainbow trout from a section of the Deschutes River that was not influenced by the stocking of hatchery rainbows, it was found that the Metolius trout have been genetically diluted and compromised by interbreeding with hatchery trout. They have lost about half or more of their resistance to "ceratomyxosis."

Of interest to anglers is the fact that attaining an extremely large size is not so much a general attribute of a species as a whole, but of a trout of particular populations of a species that have hereditary-based life histories resulting in a potential for great size. For example, the largest steelhead are those native to the Skeena River basin in British Columbia; the largest chi- nook salmon are native to the Kenai River in Alaska; the largest rainbow trout are native to Kootenay Lake and belong to a particular population that spawns in a northern tributary to the lake (the "Gerrard Kamloops" trout); the largest cut- throat trout were native to Pyramid Lake in Nevada; the world's largest brown trout occurred in the Caspian Sea, but of a single population that spawned only in the Kura River. Dams blocking spawning runs eliminated the world's largest cutthroat trout from Pyramid Lake, and the world's largest brown trout from the Caspian Sea. Although other populations of brown trout still occur in the Caspian Sea, and attain a large size, they do not attain the maximum size of the extinct Kura River population, which averaged up to thirty-three pounds in the commercial catch, with unverified maximum weights to more than one hundred pounds.

The damage done to irreplaceable units of trout diversity by the erroneous species concept of standardized interchangeable parts is well illustrated by the Pyramid Lake cutthroat trout. A Bureau of Reclamation dam effectively blocked the only spawning tributary to Pyramid Lake. The last spawning run of the native population occurred in 1938, and the average weight of those fish was twenty pounds. The world record for the species was from this population and weighed forty-one pounds, but unverified weights to sixty-two pounds were reported in a former commercial fishery.

No effort was made in 1938 to preserve a remnant of the Pyramid Lake cutthroat from extinction. Their demise was considered a sad event, but not of great import. The species, *Oncorhynchus clarki*, was not extinct, and the identical subspecies, *O. c. henshawi*, still existed in other waters of the Lahontan basin. It was assumed that any part of the species, particularly a part of the same subspecies, could be stocked into Pyramid Lake and would attain the same size as the native population. For more than forty years, millions of cutthroat trout representing the subspecies *henshawi* have been stocked into Pyramid Lake. None have reached anywhere near the maximum size of the native population. The "nonnative" Lahontan cutthroat trout lack the site-specific life-history adaptations to Pyramid Lake that were fine-tuned for thousands of generations by the native fish.

In regard to the future of our trout and salmon resources, it will be necessary for fisheries agencies to shift their emphasis from artificial propagation to natural reproduction of wild, especially wild, native fish. Mother Nature is not fooled by technological fixes.

HEAD WATERS: A CODA

Nick Lyons

It is summer and when I turn on the faucet, despite the great drought upstate, water flows easily for as long as I like, ending its stop-and-start trip from wildness to what we call civilization. I watch for a moment, stunned by this rush of clear liquid I've seen ten thousand times before, then twist the faucet until the flow diminishes, trickles, and stops. The water may have begun on some remote hillside more than a hundred miles from my kitchen, but it has come more immediately from a city reservoir not a mile from my crowded apartment, or from one no more than a couple of dozen miles upcountry.

I once fished in such a nearby body of water, unceremoniously called "Reservoir 3," chiefly because my high school friend Bernie, in Brooklyn, had it on good authority that the Canadian exhibit at the old Madison Square Garden Sportsmen's Show dumped their Atlantic salmon and ouananiche there. Bernie, our savant of stockings, was never wrong. And we were all mad to catch a ouananiche (a brand of landlocked Atlantic salmon).

We had seen them at the show one February, when, in the midst of a frozen winter, we longed for spring and the rivers that were our salvation; the fish were long, brilliantly spotted, with a bright reddish hue. There was something magical, exotic, about their name. We had caught only silvery trout, fresh from a hatchery, and these creatures from the wilderness of Canada absolutely exuded wildness. Besides, the name sounded Indian and we all wished we had that blood, or imagined we did. We tried desperately, fruitlessly, with worms, live minnows, spinning lures, and finally flies to extract even one from Reservoir 3—and in the end we had to settle for messes of crappie.

If you follow the liquid trail beyond such reservoirs—usually north, often joined by canals, pipeways, sluices, or man-made rivers to other reservoirs—you will find that in each, successively, the water is colder, the fish more beautiful. Crappie, bluegill, and perch give way to pickerel, largemouth, then smallmouth bass, which in turn, at higher elevations, become brown and rainbow trout.

The reservoirs, man-made, can provide fine sport, and so can the various waterways between them. In one such river, fed by one reservoir and running only three miles into another, I did most of my early trout fishing. It did not feel particularly artificial to me. I was a city kid and almost all flowing water was manna then. Even now, after I have fished the great chalk-streams of England and the greater spring creeks of the West, I go back to this river—and I still find in it a chance to practice certain hard-won truths, to fish over fish that have winced at scores of flies and in water that remains as familiar to me as my living room. The trout then, mostly stocked a few weeks earlier—Bernie knew to the dozen how many had been put in—brought us excitement, especially when we took a larger brown, one held over from the previous season. But we caught no ouananiche.

Above the last reservoir something else happens: the water is colder, clearer, mysterious. In one headwaters creek I know, high in the Catskill Mountains, the gradient steep and the riffles thin, everything is untouched by civilization—or, rather, continues to retreat from what is civilized. There was logging there a hundred years ago. Telephone wires connect a remote wildlife manager's cabin to the nearest town. Now and again some kids walk in, leaving their bikes three miles below. The forest is thick now, and the deadfalls tangle beneath your feet; there's no way to make a living up that way. The river there is quick and cold, even in summer. It's wilderness all right—good as you'll find this side of Labrador.

In spring spate, the river rises ten feet and takes everything in its path; I can see its marks well into the woods. In high summer, like now, its flow oozes between exposed boulders and is clear as water from a tap. The place is overhung with hemlock, willow, and birch, so that the alley of the river is intimate, shady. I have walked up there, skipping from stone to stone when the summer heat is up, in sneakers, feeling the cool water up to my calves, looking for pockets large enough to hold a trout or two, perhaps with cold seepage from a spring.

There are such pools and runs and undercut banks, and a dry fly pitched into them will bring a quick, eager spurt of water. These trout are not selective feeders; they are thoroughgoing opportunists and will take a Christmas tree of a Royal Coachman as quickly as they'll rise to a fallen ant or bug. Once I saw several large yellow stoneflies, *Perlas*, fluttering over one of the larger pools, switched to a #6 Stimulator, and caught a ten-incher, a prize in these small waters.

These are wild brook trout—five, six, sometimes eight inches, on rare occasions a foot long. They have flanks as smooth as an otter's skin, a dark mottled back, rose marks the color of wild strawberries, and striped fins. They wiggle like live jewels when you hoist them out of the water.

Greedy and wanton to their near extinction, vulnerable, full of an innocence and hunger that cannot protect itself, these fish are the ultimate emblems of piscatorial wildness, and it delights me to catch a dozen on barbless hooks and slip them swiftly back into their element. When I first climbed to the fountainhead of all city water and saw them, I stopped thinking of exotic Canadian fish and knew I had found a quiet place that satisfied my subtlest longings for that which was *not* civilized.

Little do those diminutive flashes of light and color know the fate, downriver, of the precious, pure liquid in which they flourish so unconsciously. Little do they care—so long as it is there, so long as the great cities do not drink them to extinction. They are beautiful rare creatures and they dance in my head, sustaining me, and I think of them even now, in the belly of a great gray city, during the dog days of summer, every time I turn on and turn off a faucet.

ABOUT THE CONTRIBUTORS

W. D. WETHERELL is the author of *Vermont River, North of Now, Chekhov's Sister* (a novel), *Wherever That Great Heart May Be* (short stories), and six other books. He lives in rural New Hampshire.

JOHN ENGELS has taught English Literature at St. Michael's College in Winooski, Vermont, for many years. He is the author of ten books of poetry including *Big Water* and *Weather-Fear,* for which he was a finalist for the Pulitzer Prize.

DATUS PROPER is the author of *What the Trout Said, Pheasants of the Mind,* and *The Last Old Place.* He lives on a farm in the Gallatin Valley of Montana.

JOHN GIERACH is a freelance writer living in Northern Colorado. He is a columnist for *Fly Rod & Reel* and *Sports Afield* magazines and has been the outdoor columnist for the *Longmont Daily Times-Call* in Longmont, Colorado, for the last fifteen years.

CHRISTOPHER CAMUTO is the author of *A Fly Fisherman's Blue Ridge, Another Country: Journeying Toward the Cherokee Mountains,* and the forthcoming *Hunting from Home.* He is the book review columnist for *Gray's Sporting Journal.*

TOM PALMER has been a regular contributor for *Montana Outdoors* for eleven years, and has also written for *Sports Illustrated, Buzzworm,* and several Rocky Mountain region publications. Employed by Montana Fish, Wildlife & Parks, he lives in Helena, Montana.

ROBERT J. BEHNKE is a Professor of Fishery Biology at Colorado State University. He is the author of *Native Trout of Western North America* and has been writing his own column in *Trout* magazine for fifteen years.

NICK LYONS is the author of eighteen books, most of them on fishing. He lives in New York City.